MW01181720

Are You Sleeping With The Enemy?

by

Sheri D. Smith

Unless otherwise indicated,
Scripture quotations are from the
King James Version of the Bible.

ISBN 0-9787118-0-7

Printed in the United States by
Independent Publishing Corporation
St. Louis, Missouri 63011

DEDICATION

I dedicate this book to my Lord and Savior Jesus Christ. To God be the Glory. I thank Him for His divine purpose in making me what I am today. This is not an ordinary book it is a sound from heaven. God has delivered unto me a message of urgency for His people to hear what the Spirit of God is saying to the church with warnings and truth. Thank you heavenly Father for being so gracious.

ACKNOWLEDGEMENTS

A special thanks to my father Eugene Adams, in loving memory and my wonderful loving mother, Sadie Adams for having me and for raising me. I honor and love you very much. God bless you!

Thank you for my family and friends who have been very supportive of me during the writing of this book.

A special thanks to my spiritual parents, Ministers Ernest and Jeraldine Doss. Wow! What an anointing! Thanks for planting a spiritual seed and giving me that firm spiritual foundation. Thank you for also believing in me. I honor and love you very much.

To Pastor Samuel L. Bradford for recognizing the call of God on my life. Thank you for believing in me. Thank you for the wisdom you have imparted into my life. I will always love you for that.

To Pastor and Co-Pastor, Jerome and Doris Bracely. Thank you for investing your time, energy, and interest in my life. I was blessed to be up under your anointing. For this, I am eternally grateful.

To my sneak preview readers, Princess Adams, Marla Phillips, Vickie Haynes and Delores Mays. You encouraged me in the Lord. Thank you in Jesus Name. I will never forget how we danced around in my living room giving God the Praise. Thank you Mother and Carolyn for your continuous support.

I would like to give special thanks to my sister, Princess Adams, for pushing me to finish this project. What a powerful prayer warrior! You interceded much and I thank you for all the prayers. You are a blessing. I am honored to have you as my sister.

Finally to my three loving children, Chantez (Tez), Shaquita (Ki Ki) and Deonte (Dee), thanks for believing. I love you.

INTRODUCTION

As you read this book, you are not reading for entertainment or to be amused. Be a participant. Supply your own personal experiences as you read the message. Take hold of it, struggle with it, apply it to your own life, test it, challenge it or discuss it. Involve yourself in this book.

I know someone may be asking the question, "Why did I get married?" "Why did I marry the wrong man?" "Why am I experiencing so much turmoil?" "Did I really hear from you God?" "God, do you really want me to stay single in spite of my loneliness?" "When will the right man ever come along?" "Lord, tell me why am I experiencing so much pain in my marriage?" "Lord, I am already on marriage number two, can I even handle another marriage?" "Lord, I thought my husband was saved, sanctified, and filled with the Holy Ghost, what happened?" "Listen, I am not satisfied with the husband I chose, so why do I have to stay with him?" "Is it alright to leave my husband since we are not equally yoked?"

I have asked God and even myself many of the same questions. Somebody had to go through this trauma experience so that others could be helped. So since so much mess was all around me, I was beginning to go to sleep and lose conscious of what was really surrounding me. I finally decided to call the police for help. I know the Police is in charge of maintaining Law and Order. I know He ensures the rules are followed, since He is the enforcer of the Law. I realize that He also has the power over the entire universe for the maintenance of public order, spiritual order and safety. This Police has a specialized force that ensures that regulations are obeyed. This Police has the ability to prevent crimes within a particular area.

Do you really want to know why I decided to call the Police? The reason is because I am sick and tired of being robbed so much that the devil has gotten on my last nerve! It has got to stop! He's got to give me back my stuff! I want my mind back! I want my sight and vision back! I want my peace back! I am sick of the enemy taking those things from me! I am tired of being held captive and locked up! Do you hear me? He's got to give it up! Why? Because I know someone that will help me get it back. The person that I called on happened to be none other than the Chief of Police, Jesus Christ! My God is powerful enough to unlock and loose me from the chains of bondage.

Now some of you know without a doubt that God has a specific plan for your life. As you begin to meditate on God's plan for your life, know this, God has not forgot what he told you. As long as you continue to walk in the will of God and be a doer of His word and not just a hearer, the word of God states that you will be delivered and set freeeeeeeeee from all of Satan's hindrances!

> *And the world passeth away, and the lust*
> *thereof: but he that doeth the will of God*
> *abideth forever. 1 John 2: 17*

You will be delivered and set free from all of Satan's hindrances. Don't let Satan hinder you from your destiny. Stay focused. Satan cannot keep you bound or captive for long. A lot of times when we are held captive we lose our sight or vision, but stay focused. You can be held captive on a particular job, you can be held captive in a particular relationship or even a marriage, but don't lose sight or vision. Stay focused and say to yourself, "I will not be stuck in bondage, no matter what the situation or circumstance is, because I am the righteousness of God." I hope that from my life, you can learn some things that can keep you from making similar mistakes. Let me tell you something. God is a just God, and no matter how bad the situation looks, you can always come out on top with God on your side.

Contents

SLOW DOWN

Many people don't realize that we go through things in our lives due to the many choices we make. Our life is the way it is due to the results of our choices. It is a huge responsibility to choose, but we have the right to choose. We must realize that God should be included in every decision that we make. God gave us all the right to choose and He will not take away our free will. Now we can follow the worlds' way and let the enemy influence us or we can follow Gods way and choose with wisdom. Either your choices will be foolish or your choices will be filled with wisdom. Remember that God doesn't force us to choose His way because He gives us free will to choose. God even gave us the choice to serve Him or not to serve Him. God will not force His righteousness on you. God will not force you to get saved and be born again. God will not force you to change your behavior. God does not control the choices we make. God can and will lead and guide you but the final decision is yours.

If you have been making bad decisions then you need to change your behavior. When we change our behavior, circumstances change. You cannot keep doing the same thing over and over again to get different results. You have to make the decision for yourself who you will serve. There is a wise way and a foolish way to handle any relationship whether it is on the job, at school, at your church, with your health, with your children and even in a marriage. Decisions determine your destiny. It is your choice, but I hope you choose life and not death. Let us begin making right choices and reverse the bad decisions that have been a negative impact on our lives.

You can be cursed or blessed when it comes down to your decision making. Every one of us has a choice to love life and not death. It is up to you to choose life and not death. You actually have a choice to speak life and not death. Some of us speak death all the time by being so negative. Avoid negativity! Do you know why? The reason is because you allow them to steal your peace. A negative person can also drain your spirit.

Some of us don't realize that we need to change our stinking thinking. I must seek peace and ensue it. I want to keep my joy because the joy of the Lord is my strength. As long as I allow someone to steal my joy and peace then that will weaken me. I need my strength so I can't allow that to happen. If you want to have success, then make the right decisions that God wants you to make. If God said that He was going to bless you then wait on Him. God does not need our help! Do not make the decision to help God do what He said, whether it was a prophecy, a dream, or He just spoke it to you. Wait on God because He has not forgot what He told you!

I have a question. Who chose whom in your marriage? Just because a man chooses to marry you doesn't mean you have to choose him. You are not obligated to even go out on a date with him just because he asked you and it was the nice thing to do. You better slow down and think through this thing before you decide to walk down the aisle and bust your head wide open. Yes, I know you love the attention that he gives you, but slow down. Yes, I know it feels good to you right now, but slow down. Yes, I know you are excited about the wedding rings, but slow down. Yes, I know you got the wedding bell blues, but slow down. Yes, I know you are lonely, but slow down.

Are you sure that this is the man that you can spend the rest of your life with? Are you sure that God chose this man for you? Is this person really connected to your destiny? How much do you really know about this man? Even though you are spiritual, are you choosing with your flesh or are you letting your spirit choose? Are you sure that this man can meet you in the spirit? Are you equally yoked or is this a joke? Is this man filled with the Holy Spirit, or is he even spiritual at all? Try the spirit by the spirit. Is this man a whole person and not a half or piece of a person? You need a person that is whole. Is this person just a baby that is still drinking the sincere milk? Maybe they are not mature enough for marriage yet. Maybe you are not mature enough for marriage yet.

Now it is very crucial that you answer these questions very honestly within yourself to determine if in fact you are really ready to make that big step in life. I say that because if you lie to yourself and jump into a relationship or marriage that is unholy, unhealthy and not ordained by God, honey you are going to have a battle on your hands. Do you hear me? A constant battle will be your medicine for the day. If that man is not totally ready spiritually, he can hurt you in many ways. So all you have to do is be truthful with yourself. This could keep you from heartache and pain. So I am asking you in the name of Jesus Christ, to take your time, evaluate the situation and just slow down! Why are you in such a hurry anyway? Promise God that from this day forward, you will make up in your mind to choose wisely and stick to it. Don't let anyone persuade you. Don't be moved by what other people have to say about the situation. Don't be moved by what he or she looks like.

Don't settle for less when you are Gods' best. The wrong decision can cost you an arm and a leg (slang for a lot), if you are not careful. Remember ladies, whoever you decide to choose for marriage, you are commanded to submit to him. So if you got the blind leading you, then you may just fall into a ditch right along with him. Wake up and check it out thoroughly.

Take your time and slow down when you choose your friends also. So many of us get messed up trying to fit in with a particular crowd or click and you don't fit. You don't fit and they don't fit. Your particular lifestyle does not fit with theirs. So it shows because you stick out. Don't try to fit into a particular click. Now don't get me wrong. God will sometimes allow you to witness to someone worldly on a regular basis for a season, but when that season is up you must move on.

Proverbs 12: 26 states that the righteous should choose their friends carefully. And don't try to fool anybody by saying that you are trying to bring them into the fold, when your lifestyle is showing us that they are pulling you into the worldly fold. The wicked will do nothing but lead you astray, so stay focused and slow down. Please be careful whom you hang out with. Ask yourself, "What do we have in common?" If who you are hanging out with is causing you to slip, dip and trip into sin then stop hanging out with them! Of course God may remove them anyway if you don't. Remember that evil communication can corrupt good manners.

So choose to be around the highest quality of people you can. Choose the ones whose hearts are focused or aimed toward God. Some of us just call anybody our friend and that can be dangerous. Some of your so-called friends may smile in your face and yet stab you in your back. What I mean by that is that your so-called friend may act like they like you but in fact they really don't so they may talk about you behind your back to put you down. A true friend doesn't act like that.

A true friend can see the real you without all the makeup and not turn around and talk about you or put you down because you hold a certain position or title. Some people that act like this are sometimes jealous of who you are and want what you have. They may even want to be you.

> *Be not unequally yoked together*
> *wth unbelievers.*
> *2 Corinthians 6: 14*

This doesn't mean we can never be around people, who are not Christians, but our closest most influential relationships should be with people who know and love the Lord with all their heart, or there will be consequences. If you continue to be connected or joined together with unbelievers all the time, then either you will pull them or they will pull you. So be very careful who you keep company with. I thank God for saving me and changing me! This is one thing I know for sure, God is not finished with me yet. As for me in my house, we will serve the Lord, but I am not going to isolate myself from unbelievers because they don't believe the way I believe. I am going to continue to let my light shine in the midst.

Now we all got some haters, but it is good to know who they are so that you can watch and pray. Don't let the enemy steal your peace. Yes people are going to talk about you. They talked about Jesus and he did no wrong. Just keep living, you will be talked about whether you like it or not. But don't let this stop you from doing the right thing. Just because I sit and eat with sinners does not make me a sinner. I don't see how people think that they can get away from sinners totally anyway. We are sinners saved by grace ourselves and we can't get away from our own self.

There are sinners in the church. Are you going to stop going to church because there are sinners there? There are sinners in the grocery store. Are you going to stop buying groceries because there are sinners working and shopping there? There are sinners in your family. Are you going to stop going around your family members because sinners are there? There are sinners on the streets and highways. Are you going to stay off the streets, roads or highways because sinners are there? There are sinners in the shopping malls and department stores. Are you going to stop shopping because sinners are there?

What makes you think that you are better than anybody else that you cannot be around sinners. Hate the sin but not the sinner. Now if being around sinners cause you to sin then yes you need to come from among them. Now if you are married to an unbeliever, then you are not to come from among them all because they didn't squeeze the toothpaste from the bottom. That is not stealing your peace. This is not a legal reason for divorce.

Chapter 1
LOVE NOT SLEEP!

Before you began to read the text and its entirety, let me inform you of something very crucial. Some of us seem to think in our minds after being in one bad relationship after another, that those people whom we had the bad relationships with becomes the enemy. Some people think their husband or wife is the enemy when in fact they are not. They think that their children, family, co-workers, and even their Pastors are the enemy when in fact they are not. Listen, these people are not the enemy, but each one of these people can be influenced greatly by the enemy. Please understand that even though someone has hurt you in the past, whether it is your husband, wife, Pastor, business partner, co-worker, friend or whoever, they should not be considered to be the enemy.

Jesus welcomed prostitutes, tax collectors and other sinners into the Kingdom of God. The Pharisees and the Scribes murmured and accused Jesus for eating with sinners. Jesus did not view the sinners as our enemies. Jesus described the Pharisees as the children of the devil in the book of John. In the book of Matthew Jesus described them as the blind leading the blind. Jesus also called the Scribes hypocrites. Listen, just because their lifestyle is in opposition to our lifestyle does not mean that they are the enemy. On one of my jobs, I used to play dominos or cards with co-workers who's lifestyle was in opposition to mine, but that didn't stop me from sitting with them. They are not my enemy. All I would do is continue to let my light shine. There was a burden in my heart for each one of them and their families because of the love I have for them. I had to keep in mind that I can't change them but God can. I can't even change myself the way I need to be changed but God can.

The church house should welcome sinners just as Jesus did and stop talking about them so badly. Now someone that is blind like the Pharisees may talk about you. Also someone that is a hypocrite like the Scribes may talk about you. Let them talk because they talked about Jesus. Now this does not mean we should compromise with them, because as a matter of fact we should not. Our Pastors should welcome a sinner in the church house but teach them not to compromise the word of God. We must be transformed by the renewing of our mind. I say that because we are all sinners saved by grace. We must not be people pleasers but we should be God pleasers. Now the enemy would love to put you in sleep mode. In fact the enemy would love to sleep with you. Warning! You should not be sleeping with the enemy! Are you sleeping with the enemy? Why do I say that? I'll tell you why, because it will make you lazy. It will also make you poor and blind. To top it off, you will never be satisfied because there will always be a hunger for more.

> *Love not sleep, lest thou come*
> *to poverty, open thine eyes, and*
> *thou shalt be satisfied with bread.*
> *Proverbs 20: 13*

Listen, don't starve yourself and miss out on Gods best by sleeping so much. Some people don't care whose bed they are sleeping in. As a matter of fact, some will sleep around everywhere. I don't know about you but I don't have a feeling of safety when I am sleeping in the wrong bed. I also don't have a feeling of safety when the wrong person is sleeping in my bed. The scripture plainly tells us that we should not love sleeping. Now we all know that the human body has to have natural rest and sleep in order to restore itself. This scripture is not speaking of this type of physical or natural sleep that we need in order to function properly. It is actually speaking of indolent sleep.

What is indolent sleep? Indolent sleep is being lazy and not showing any interest or making any effort to live a better life. When you are lazy like that then you become painless and slow to change. It doesn't bother you that you sleep around. It doesn't bother you that you go from house to house chasing prophecies trying to get a word or trying to fulfill a need. You have become immune to pain. It doesn't bother you that you are not working to better your life because if it did, then you would change. When you become lazy like that then you become insensitive to pain even though you suffer. I'd like to call it a disease or condition that is slow to develop or be healed.

You must seek God for yourself and stop chasing prophecies because a prophetic word is just confirmation for what God has already told you in most cases. If you are always seeking a word, then you must be careful. Why? The reason is because the enemy would love to slip in there to give you a word to destroy you, your family and friends. All prophecies are not from God. I repeat, all prophecies are not from God. Why do you say that? It is because there is such a thing called false prophecy. Wake up and stop being so lazy and begin to seek God for yourself.

So do you think after sleeping so much that it causes you no pain? If you think that then you are wrong. I like to call it the silent killer. Love not sleep! You need to open your eyes so that you won't live in poverty. When the bible speaks of poverty, it is speaking of near starvation. It is the state of being poor. It is the state of not having enough money to take care of your basic needs such as food, clothing and housing. It is simply living in lack of material and spiritual well being. As long as you stay in the state of being lazy then you will be deprived of your benefits. Your basic way or standard of living will cause you to be disadvantaged. This disease or condition called indolent sleep or laziness will affect you. We must learn to escape a relationship that has no hope but causes much pain.

Open your eyes and discern (distinguish, recognize, identify, detect or come to know) the destroyer. You need to know who and what you are dealing with because people perish for the lack of knowledge. If you don't recognize who the destroyer really is then let me say that he (the enemy) will try to kill you. He will try to steal from you. He will try to destroy you. Don't give up the goods like that. Don't even waste time like that. You should not waste time on someone who is always trying to get revenge for something someone said or did. Why do I say that? I say that because the bible clearly states, "Vengeance is mine said the Lord." You could actually mess yourself up by putting matters into your own hands. You can cause a delay in reaching your destiny while trying to put a hold on someone else's destiny. Why do I say that? I say that because if you put your mouth on Gods anointed or hurt them in any kind of way then this could cause you trouble. Now they may not talk the way you think they should talk or they may not walk the way you think they should walk but who are you? The bible states to touch not my anointed and do my prophets no harm. Now this doesn't mean that Gods anointed will not make some mistakes, but it will be in your best interest to let God handle the situation.

You are not God! So if you decide to take matters into your own hands anyway then don't say that you were not warned. My advice to you today is to "Slow Down and WAKE UP!"

Chapter 2
WHO ARE YOU?

Do you really know who you are? Do you really know whom you belong to? That is the problem today. Some of you don't really know who you really are and why you were created. It's not about you! Yes we are human beings whether it is male or female. God created us. We were created for God's glory and only the creator can reveal your purpose. We were made in Gods image. We were made upright. We are endowed with intelligence. We are fearfully and wonderfully made.

We were given wide dominion. You are superior to animals whether they are four legged, two legged or don't have any legs at all. We are male and female. You are the living being. Man was formed from the dust but when God breathed into him life he became a living soul. Men and women of God, you are a spirit and you posses a soul while you are yet in the physical body. The spirit man is the real you. You must have a spirit led life in God. Only allow your life to be governed by the truth and the word of God is truth.

Before Eve ever came on the scene everything was created and she was covered. Eve didn't have to wonder how they were going to live or what were they going to eat. There were divine supplies. Before the wife even came into the picture man was given vision and direction from God. The bible says, "without a vision the people perish." Adam was already working and being trained before his wife even came to reality. She was already covered.

Genesis 2: 18 reads, "And the Lord God said, it is not good that the man should be alone, I will make him a help meet for him." God said I would make. God is saying let me help you choose. God is saying let me have say. God is saying let me appoint somebody for the role of a wife or husband. Why? The reason is because He knows the necessary qualities that are needed to meet your needs. For instance, what if your daddy said that he was going to come to your house and make you a cake? Now deep down inside you know that he is very good at baking. You know that daddy has a reputation of making the best cakes that you have ever tasted. He knows the necessary ingredients needed to make the best cake that you have ever tasted. Well, daddy hadn't made it to your house yet while you were waiting and you got impatient. You decided to make the cake on your own. Well, needless to say, the cake was missing some very special ingredients. So since you made the cake anyway without waiting on daddy, you messed it up. Wait on daddy before you try to do it on your own baby!

Genesis 2: 21 reads, "And the Lord God caused a deep sleep to fall upon Adam, and he slept and he took one of his ribs, and closed up the flesh instead thereof;" God took one rib and not two or three. That means that one woman is sufficient men. Now the rib came out of his side and not his back. That means that you are to walk side by side with your spouse and not in front of. I remember when my spouse and I would be walking from our car going somewhere. He would always walk ahead of me. I would ask him to wait on me. His excuse to me was that I walk to slow. I thought that was very rude. He would act like he was rushing to leave me behind. Men, your wife is considered to be part of your body. She is considered to be your own flesh and bones. That's why Adam said that she is bone of my bone and flesh of my flesh. Now you have become one flesh. There is one important thing that people are missing from this scripture. When God took one of Adams ribs then his wife Eve came. The important point is that God closed his flesh. Adams flesh had to be shut down to realize that it is not all about just him anymore. You have a wife now. Respect her and don't be selfish and controlling! Likewise ladies respect your husband and don't you be selfish and controlling either!

Men if your wife is considered to be part of your own body, then surely you won't hurt her because you would be hurting your own body. God also caused Adam to fall into a deep sleep, which caused Adam to die to self. Adam had to die to self before his wife came. Listen ladies, I know you don't want a selfish or self-will man for your husband. There is nothing worse than marrying a selfish or a self-will man. Now there is a difference when God puts you to sleep versus when the enemy puts you to sleep. When God puts you to sleep then you will awake with vision. God wants you to awake with understanding of who you are and why you were created. He wants you to awake with purpose. You will be naked and not ashamed. On the other hand, when the enemy puts you to sleep, he never wants you to awake. The enemy wants you to stay in sleep mode without understanding of who you really are. The enemy wants you to be unconscious and unlearned about your purpose in life.

Once Eve became Adams wife, the bible states that they were naked and not ashamed. To be naked and not ashamed in this case shows a sign of innocence. The innocence of being free from guilt and sin. It is when you lose your innocence that disobedience and idolatry is present. The kind of innocence that should be present in your life and marriage is that you should walk in and obey the will of God. You must have morals. You both should be spiritual in order for the marriage to be successful. You should have values. You should respect one another and build one another up. Most of all you should allow God to govern your life.

We as human beings are people viewed especially as having imperfections and weaknesses. We are human beings. So with our imperfections we have faults, we have defects, we lack completeness and we are not perfect, right? We will always lack completeness without God. We will always lack completeness when we lose our innocence. With our weaknesses there is a character flaw. There is a lack of strength. There is a lack of power. There is a lack of determination. There will always be a character flaw and lack of strength if we won't rest in God. There will always be a character flaw and lack of strength when you walk in disobedience. The flesh will always cause us to have weaknesses if we don't allow God to put the flesh to sleep. We must die to the flesh daily.

When we are weak we can find ourselves being fond of something due to our fleshly desires. We could have a strong liking for something that could throw us off course. For instance, if you continue to feel sorry for yourself then this could throw you off course or cause a delay in reaching your destiny. Now there is nothing wrong with a prophetic word but if you continue to chase prophecies then this could throw you off course. We could really lose our focus and purpose due to a weakness. For instance, you could have a weakness for chocolate covered strawberries and I could have a weakness for a high yellow good looking man with natural curly hair, not realizing that either one could be rotten on the inside. Be careful what you crave. Whatever your weakness is, when you approach it or come near it then you tend to act a little strange or act out of your normal character. You might even get clumsy and trip over something. We give our own self away. Our weakness becomes an object of desire or an irresistible object of desire. If this is you then come out of denial and REPENT!

Now your weakness may be love stories that cause you to cry so much. Maybe it is lifetime movies. Have you noticed that when you watch one lifetime movie you find yourself getting stuck? It becomes hard for you to stop watching one after another because your focus has been thrown off. Yes your focus can be thrown off for crying so much. Watch it when you tend to get emotional a lot. Why do you say that? I say that because emotions are a weapon for the enemy. Whatever the case may be that could be throwing you off course, please don't get stuck and become unconscious of your surroundings.

Don't place yourself in sleep mode with the enemy and get stuck to the point of becoming lazy. The reason I say that is because when you become lazy, you tend to become weak in many areas. Now there is nothing wrong with a prophetic word but beware when a person is supposed to be operating out of the prophetic and always got a word for you every time that they see you. Stop trying to chase down a prophetic word and continue to seek God for yourself. Don't be so lazy! Come out of denial and REPENT!

When we speak of the word weak the dictionary describes it as not being physically or mentally strong. In some cases our weaknesses can drain us physically and mentally if we keep falling for it. (This is a temporary state.) Being weak also states that we can be easily defeated, we lack strength of character and we may be lacking skills, abilities or talents. For instance, some of us lack the ability to hear from God because we are not seeking his face and studying his word for ourselves.

Some of us think that going to church on Sunday morning is enough. Honey, it is going to take more than Sunday morning service to get an understanding of Gods word.

Some of us are made weak and tired by extreme heat and exhaustion. For instance, if you are in a relationship with someone who is constantly playing games with you then this could cause extreme heat or physical exertion. If they are putting you down all the time then this could cause extreme heat or physical exertion. If they are disrespecting you and just constantly abusing you, then after so long you will eventually get weak and tired from all this. This becomes extreme heat or physical exertion. Some of us have over exerted ourselves. We have exercised so much from relationship to relationship that we may never have to go to the gym ever again. Hello somebody! Some of us have had on the job training. Some of you have picked up a skill or talent and have not realized it yet.

A skill in most cases requires training and experience to do well. When you become skilled or gifted, you are characterized with a special ability. Why? It is because you have had practice over time. Now if you keep it real and admit before you actually picked up a skill or gift that you have made some mistakes, then God can anoint you to be very gifted in this area. Not only will God gift or anoint you in this area, He will also use you to teach others so that they can learn from the mistakes you have made. Now some of us take longer to learn than others because of our one-track minds or our hard headedness. After you have messed up time and time again then you should have enough intelligence that has equipped you with enough information not to fall for any stupidity or mess ever again. At least in that area you should have learned. I myself have learned after messing up time and time again.

Why do you say that? I say that because it is not really about how skilled or anointed I am, but it is about if it had not been for the Lord on my side, I wouldn't be here today! If it had not been for God, I wouldn't even have a skill. I wouldn't even have a gift. I wouldn't even have an anointing.

Maybe you never had to train for anything because you had awakened knowing everything. If this is you then maybe this book is not for you. I have never met anyone that knows it all or have attained it all. Are you always tip toeing through the tulips? Yes we are human but we all need the help of the Lord to succeed in life. Listen, if God is going to do a work in your life then guess what, experience could be the best teacher. Surely there are a lot of jobs that requires experience. God will allow you to get the experience to put you in a particular place. Remember your choices put you in a lot of these places. Some people call it the wilderness experience. Now some of us do have a natural ability to do something well. This is considered to be a talent but if God is not in it then it will not be anointed. If you think that you know it all, then that means that you have arrived. I don't think so! So please stop being so judgmental! Some people are so quick to judge any and everybody. Some will even judge people with titles.

> *Ephesians 4: 11, 12*
> *And he gave some, apostles; and some,*
> *prophets; and some, evangelists; and*
> *some, pastors and teachers; (verse 11)*
>
> *For the perfecting of the saints, for the*
> *work of the ministry, for the edifying*
> *of the body of Christ. (verse 12)*

Now some people hold a position out of the diversity of spiritual gifts. Even though they hold one of these positions, they are humans also with imperfections. Yes it is true that these gifts should be used for the perfecting of the saints. It should be used for the work of the ministry. It should be used to edify the body of Christ. Now it didn't say edify YOU or ME but it did say to edify the body of Christ. These gifts are to be used to mature the people of God. I remember when I saw my Pastor at the time make some mistakes that hurt me to my heart. I was putting him up on a pedestal. When I saw what he did, it sort of hindered my walk in God. The reason is because I thought Pastors are supposed to be perfect or at least almost perfect. I learned that they are humans also with imperfections. God showed me while there are many great leaders, there are also many leaders that are unlearned and stuck in tradition which makes the word of God of no affect. Please pray for our Leaders! Pray for them all across the nation. Why should we pray for them? The reason is because the enemy is after our Leaders and we do not want the body of Christ to die in the process of them dying.

Now there are some cases where people in leadership think that they are more important than God. Some think that they are more important than you. Some leaders will not listen to anybody else because they believe that they know it all and you cannot teach them anything. Why? It is because they have and UN-teachable spirit. Honey, you can even learn from a baby. These are the leaders that look for the people to lift them up rather than God. Honey, you need to wake up and realize that it is not about you, nor your title. I remember a young lady that I knew once that became a pastor of a local church. I hadn't seen her in awhile, but one day she visited the church that I was attending at the time which was the same church that she attended years ago. Well, when she came in, I tried to introduce her to my husband and I called her by her first name. What did I do that for? Well needless to say, she corrected me. She said, "It is reverend." I then said, "Well excuse me please." She then said, "It is about the preliminaries." Honey, it is not about you or your title. It is about lifting up God. It is about pleasing God rather than man. Your title does not validate who you really are in God. You think too highly of yourself. Who are you? Are you bearing any fruit that is good to eat? If not, then I don't want to eat it!

Do not let the enemy cause a character assassination. When the enemy try to kill you it is a deliberate and sustained attack on your reputation. He is deliberately trying to set you back because he wants you to experience injury, damage, loss or defect. From the beginning of time there has been an attack on the family. It's time to wake up and declare war against Satan. It is time to take back what the enemy has stolen from you. The enemy was running game on Eve back in the day since the beginning of time to take her focus off of what God had planned for her life.

Adam and Eve was doing fine until the serpent (the enemy) came on the scene. Adam and Eve were doing just fine in the Garden of Eden until Satan allured and tempted Eve. The snake distracted her. How many snakes have you allowed in your life to distract you? Stop eating the fruit that the snake keeps offering you. Because Eve let Satan trick her into eating the forbidden fruit then sorrow will be greatly multiplied. So if some of you are wondering why you are going through so much sorrow, then maybe you ate the fruit that was forbidden. I believe that Eve became dazed by the temptation because the enemy made it look good to her. How many times have you let someone's words put you into a trance? I believe that the enemy put Eve to sleep with the fruit of conversation he gave her, which caused her to fall or make a bad decision. She made a bad choice and had to reap the consequences.

Why do we allow the enemy to come into our house? Now the garden is a protected and cultivated place. God revealed to me that Eden was the very first home that we need to take note of. Adam and Eve allowed the enemy to come into their home. Now Eden is also called the garden of God. You are to delight yourself in the garden of God where there is a protected place. When there is a cultivating place in God then delight yourself but do not allow the enemy to come into your garden or house (Eden) and destroy what God has joined together. Do not invite the enemy into your house!

What therefore God hath joined
together, let not man put asunder.
Mark 10: 9

I don't know about you but I don't want to get a divorce or even cause a divorce if God joined you together. I do not want to be penalized for separating what God has joined together. We see what happened in Adam and Eve's house. God joined them together. They allowed the enemy to slip into their home with temptation and they fell for it even though God joined them together. Stop letting your family and friends dictate how your household should be ran. You need to know for yourself once you evaluate the relationship whether God joined you together or not. One thing for sure, I don't want to be joined together with anyone that God had no part in.

The enemy was probably filling Eve's head with all types of compliments that seemed so convincing and she fell for it. Maybe some of the compliments were even true but what was his motive behind it? People wake up and see that the enemy is trying to run game on us today just like he did yesterday. Some of us silly women let men captivate us with all the compliments. Don't let it go to your head sweetheart. You are supposed to know who you are in God and stand on that even before the enemy approaches you with words or compliments. Don't you dare get drunk off of the compliments. Do not let them seduce or persuade you into doing wrong. We are not having it because we are getting fit and in shape to handle whatever the enemy brings our way.

> *And I will put enmity between thee*
> *and the woman, and between thy*
> *seed and her seed, it shall bruise thy*
> *head, and thou shall bruise his heel.*
> *Genesis 3: 15*

Let me help you with something. The enemy is known for messing with your head. The enemy will always try to confuse you and bring division between you and your head. But God gave us power over the enemy to bruise his head. You need to know this. The enemy will use somebody to whip circles around your head with compliments. That's why you have a lot of married people cheating today. Be careful ladies because the enemy may try to come through you to get to your head by using the babysitter. Beware of the slicksters. Now there is nothing wrong with compliments but don't get drunk off of the compliments. Don't let it go to your head because you may find yourself sleepwalking or in a daze because of all the words or compliments. If this occurs, then when you finally awake, you may ask yourself, what happened? How did that happen? How did I get there? When did that happen?

What happened was that you got drunk. You got so drunk off the words or compliments and now you can't figure out how you got in that sleeping position with the enemy. One day the compliments tasted so smooth. The next time it tasted like he mixed the compliments with a little salt. He was trying to give it a little flavor. Finally he went in for the kill and topped it off with a little juice. Yes it got so juicy to you that you got drunk and ended up in bed with him.

You need to know that you don't have to drink alcohol only to get drunk. When you get drunk in this case, while being influenced by the enemy, you are under the influence of a demonic spirit such as witchcraft. Now when you get drunk like that, you will become controlled. Why? The reason is because the enemy has a controlling spirit. When you get drunk your speech will become slurred. You will begin to speak without understanding. Your vision becomes blurred. You think you can see but your vision becomes fuzzy and you can't see clearly. Remember the bible states, "without a vision the people perish." That's why you have so many unholy and unhealthy relationships. That is why you have so many women in relationships with married men today. They got drunk, they couldn't see and so they went to sleep.

That is when the unexpected bruises come. I am speaking of an emotional injury. The enemy will play on your emotions. I am talking about an injury that is not physical, although the physical injuries could come also. I am talking about an emotional injury that will cause hurt feelings or even damage your self-esteem. I'm speaking of SCARS! You need to know that bruises do take some time to heal. A relational bruise can crush you. It can also cause you to get upset. Why will it cause you to get upset? The reason is because your feelings will be injured and your self-esteem will be harmed. Why? The reason is because the whole relationship was a lie in the first place. They have been lying to you from the start.

In many cases you become addicted to the relationship and never want to depart or end it even though it is not good for you. You may even become a fool for that person while the enemy is influencing you.

There are some cases when a person will give all their money just to get a word or a compliment. Don't put yourself out there like that. If you get caught up in a relationship like this, and you don't except the warnings then something will happen to you. What happens is that you will become stubborn, rebellious, selfish, self-indulging, proud, conceited, arrogant, boastful and unchangeable. This happens all because you wouldn't listen and take heed to the warnings. Your sorrow will then become greatly multiplied. As if that is not enough to mess you up! If God gives you a warning to kill a relationship then if you won't kill it then it will kill you.

> *And take heed to yourselves, lest at*
> *any time your hearts be overcharged*
> *with surfeiting (overindulgence in*
> *something especially in food or drink),*
> *and drunkenness, and cares of this life,*
> *and so that day come upon you unawares.*
> *Luke 21: 34*

The enemy tried to kill you with the words and compliments. I came to tell you that the enemy couldn't kill you because God had his hands on you. The only thing the enemy could do is put you to sleep. He loves to play mind games, but enough is enough! The enemy will be defeated. You were just sleeping. Sure you made some stupid mistakes but what else is new? You were just resting and fell asleep in the wrong bed. We will awake even though most of us have spent a period of time sleeping.

We assume a position at night that is different from the daytime position. People seem to sleep better when it's dark in their life and they can't see. When the sunrises they tend to wake up. We may not realize it but a lot of us have been put to sleep by the enemy. The enemy even provided the bed for us to sleep in. He wants us to remain in sleep mode so we can go straight to hell and live in hell. Psalm 139: 8 reads, "If I ascend up into heaven, thou art there: if I make my bed in hell, behold, thou art there." God is omnipresent and He will meet you where you are even if you are living in hell. All you have to do is call on Him for help. Wake up! Stop sleeping with the enemy! Let the Son of God arise in your life. Let God bring light to your situation!

That's why we should be very concerned about our family members and friends salvation. If they depart from this earth today, their salvation determines whether they will go to Heaven or Hell. The enemy will love for you or anybody else to die without Christ. Listen if you die in Christ, that means that you will eventually wake up because you are just sleep in Jesus. You are just sleeping temporarily. God can comfort you during this trying time just call on Him. God has resurrection power, so you need to know that you shall rise again because there is life after death when you die in Christ.

> *I Thessalonians 4: 13-18*
> *But I would not have you to be ignorant,*
> *brethren, concerning them which are*
> *asleep, that ye sorrow not, even as others*
> *which have no hope. (verse 13)*
>
> *For if we believe that Jesus died and rose*
> *again, even so them also which sleep in*
> *Jesus will God bring with him. (verse 14)*

19

*For this we say unto you by the word of the
Lord, that we which are alive and remain
unto the coming of the Lord shall not prevent
them which are asleep. (verse 15)*

*For the Lord himself shall descend from
heaven with a shout, with the voice of the
archangel, and with the trump of God, and
the dead in Christ shall rise first. (verse 16)*

*Then we which are alive and remain shall
be caught up together with them in the
clouds, to meet the Lord in the air, and so
shall we ever be with the Lord. (verse 17)*

*Wherefore comfort one another with these
words. (verse 18)*

Did you know that by comforting someone in Gods word could give them relief from pain and anxiety? For those followers of Christ who died or been put to sleep, you need to understand that there is hope. Yes there is eternal hope but you must keep the faith and believe that you can rise again. If you fall, then get back up again.

So even though you may be in a dead relationship and been through days of tribulation, when it is time to rise, God will give you a sound from heaven. You will hear the sound of the trumpet of God. That sound is an alert that Christ is coming to handle your situation. None of us know the day or the hour that He will come, but one thing we do know is that He is coming. God will raise you from the dead.

Don't be like the people during the time of Noah that wasn't ready. They continued to live their lives the way that they wanted to out of ignorance. They even laughed at Noah and talked about him but Noah heard from God and obeyed His instructions. When God say it is time, then it is time. If you are not ready when the time comes then you will continue to burn forever. It will be so clear to you when God gives you instructions as long as you acknowledge Him. He may say Lazarus, come forth! He may say Lazarus come out! I know you know the story of how Jesus raised Lazarus from the dead.

The name Lazarus means, one whom God helps. You need to know that God will help you in a time of trouble. But you need to search yourself and find out who and where you are in God. Are you walking in obedience? If not then God is calling you out of darkness into the marvelous light. It is a divine call. When God calls you please don't try to hide like Adam did. God asked Adam where are you? When Adam heard the divine call from God he tried to hide himself. The reason he hid himself is because he was walking in disobedience. So he gave God an excuse by shifting the blame. Listen, don't blame anyone else for your own disobedience. Don't blame your husband, don't blame your wife, don't blame your children, don't blame your Pastor or anyone else for your own disobedience. I remember a time in my life when I was blaming my husband for my actions. I blamed him for me walking in disobedience. Listen, I cannot blame my husband for my own disobedience. It was my own fault that I chose to walk in disobedience and not my husband.

It does not matter what your spouse is doing to you but it does matter how you respond. The question is how do you respond? He didn't make me do it. I made what I thought was a conscious decision to walk in disobedience. I didn't realize at the time that the enemy was putting me in sleep mode. I was in sleep mode and didn't even realize it. I wanted to point the finger at my spouse for ruining my life when he didn't do it. I did it to myself.

One day you will die. Either you will die in Christ or die in sin. Hopefully you will die in Christ so that you can rise again and live eternally. Hopefully you will die to your flesh. When God calls you then just come out of your sin. When you hear that great sound from heaven then come out of your addiction. Come out of your bondage. Come out of your depression. Come out of your sickness and disease. Come out of your fear. Come out of your poverty. Come out of condemnation. Come out of your blindness. Come out of the abuse. Come out of the deep sleep. Lazarus, come out! There is life after death!

Just when the devil thought it was over, the Lord turned the page in your life. This is not how your story ends. Why do you say that? I say that because you are going to wake up and see the light. I say that because you are going to wake up and stop sleeping with the enemy. You are going to realize who you really are and determine your purpose in life. It's not over! Soon your fear, torment and agony will be over. If you really get a hold to this then soon your blindness and injustice will be over. Listen your marriage may be messed up but it's not over for you. Your child may be messed up but it's not over. You may have been terminated from your job but it's not over. Your finances may be messed up right now but it's not over. Your life may be messed up right now but it's not over for you. You shall live and not die! God I pray deliverance in the lives of your people right now! I thank you God for the victory!

Listen, God wants us to be conscious of His word. On the other hand, the enemy wants you to be partially or fully unconscious. The enemy wants you to walk around like you just don't have a clue. He wants you to feel dumb and be dumber. He wants you to think that you have no purpose in life. That's why we have some people killing themselves before they receive God into their life. They have been put to sleep by the enemy and they fell for it. A lot of times what causes us to be put to sleep is from past hurts, pain, traumas, tragedy, disease, blindness, loneliness, abuse, health challenges, etc. Watch it when you start to feel so lonely. You will look for compliments from anybody and the enemy could be setting you up. Let's keep it real. I used to look for men to compliment me all the time but since I know who I am in God then that doesn't bother me anymore. Now let me say it again. There is nothing wrong with prophecies but trust me God knows how to get a word to you even if He has to send them to your house. You should never chase prophecies because the enemy could easily slip in there somewhere to mislead you or deceive you. Don't you dare give him the victory. Let us thank God for the true prophets of God. I said let us thank God for the true prophets of God!

Listen, I am no better than you. I am one of you who was hurting and didn't know how to get out of a dead relationship. But if God can bring me out then God can bring you out also. My best days are ahead of me now. The bible states that my sorrow will be multiplied. It was multiplied because I made a bad choice by eating the forbidden fruit. I allowed someone to become the apple of my eye that wasn't right for me. Listen very closely. Every relationship is not meant to build up. I was trying to build on a relationship that wasn't meant to build up. I was in love with the attention that I was getting. I wanted words and compliments. That put me in a dangerous state. Now there is nothing wrong with words and compliments. But let me say this, if it is coming from someone that is operating in the wicked realm and you begin to believe and receive it to be true, then there is something wrong with that. The devil is a liar!

The bible states that in sorrow you shall bring forth children. In other words, if you get out of the wrong relationship safely, after you heard the sound from heaven, then you shall bring forth children. What children are you speaking of? The children could be your ministry, your book, your musical CD, your home, your business, wisdom and knowledge, etc. These are things that you could give birth to after your sorrow or misery. Your misery becomes your ministry anyway. The best is yet to come. It doesn't matter where you've been or what you have done, God has a plan for your life. You were born for Gods purpose. It does not yet appear what God has in store for you. Yes you can start all over again because God got your back. You need to know that you know that you know who you are in God.

Weight Watchers

Be careful to watch the weight that you put on. You should become a member of the weight watchers program. If you decide to join or become a member of the weight watchers program then you must weigh in every week. That way you can find out how much weight you have lost or gained. Now if you are working out throughout the week, then you will begin to lose some kind of weight. After so long, some parts of the body should be built up. Now don't be like some of the people who are trying to build for nothing. If you are not eating properly then it won't work. How can you build anything or lose any weight if you keep eating junk? How are you eating at home? You can use this same principal in a marriage. In order to have a successful marriage you must eat properly. What are you eating at home? What are you being fed? Are you being fed love, kindness, peace, joy and respect? If so, then you are eating from the smart ones and you get points for that. If not then maybe you are being fed junk food like disrespect, name calling, lying, cheating or abuse. If you are constantly eating junk food then your marriage will not be successful. Remember, some relationships are not meant to build up.

Some of us have been in weight training. Some of us are trying to lift weights on a constant basis. Be careful because you might hurt your back from lifting so much and this could put you on bed rest. We all need to be trained properly. We are all in training right now. But while we are in training we will find that the weights are used to strengthen the muscles. This is a part of our exercise. Some of us are in tiptop shape when it comes to dealing with the weights of this world. I am speaking of things such as unhealthy relationships, sickness, violent attitude, abuse, trauma, tragedy, loneliness, etc.

So since you have joined the weight watchers program then you need to know their trademark. Their trademark is an organization that help people who want to lose the weight. Listen, God will help those who want to be helped. Do you really want to lose the weight that you put on yourself? Do you really have determination? Are you really motivated? If so, then we need to stop making so many bad choices about the food that we choose to eat starting today. Now we need to determine how much weight have you really been lifting each week, each month and each year.

Every house that is governed by God should have a weight watchers program so you can lose some excess weight. When you say lose the weight what weight are you talking about? I'm speaking of the heaviness or certain issues of life. Your heaviness or issues of life need to be measured. When you first start this program you must weigh in to find out the specific amount a person weighs. Just last week you could have gained weight in the area of mental burden, oppression, depression, lust, lying, jealousy, abuse, etc.

How much weight have you gained since last week and in what area? Whatever the excessive weight is that you put on, you need to watch it so that you don't get fat off of it. Why? It is because some foods are very fattening and addictive. That is not good for you. Too much weight is not good for you. In some cases not having enough weight is not good for you either. It can be unhealthy for you either way. You need to eat a balance meal and have a balance life. When you lose weight you are not to gain any while watching it very closely.

You also need to build in order to gain strength. You cannot gain strength by not eating properly. As a matter of fact, you will get tired of eating junk after awhile. Why? The reason is because you will begin to see how much weight it is putting on you and you will get tired of looking at it. You will get tired of carrying it around. You will get sick and tired of feeling tired. You will begin to say to yourself, enough is enough! So since your body is under construction then you will need the necessary tools to build or you will break down. You don't want to fall apart so make sure you are using the proper equipment then your strength will come. Don't over do it now.

You should ask yourself, "How important is it for me to lose the weight?" If you are getting fat off of excess weight then that mean you have an unrestrained behavior. In fact if you have no restraints, then this could cause you not to be equipped enough to carry the weight. This could cause you to strain yourself so be very careful. Don't make a move to soon. Don't over exert yourself. There may be no restraints because you will not control yourself. I Corinthians 9: 27 reads, "But I keep under my body, and bring it into subjection: lest that by any means, when I have preached to others, I myself should be a castaway."

First of all, let us all come out of self-denial. We all need some self control somewhere in our lives. And we all need to restrain some of our appetites. Control your appetite! Maybe you talk about people too much and judge them all the time, when your life is not the picture of good health either. You need some self-control. You need to restrain your appetite from putting people down so much. Remember you will reap what you sow. There are no restraints because you won't control yourself. You must restrain yourself from chasing prophecies. Control yourself! Listen, if God gave you a word to separate yourself from your friend for a season then that doesn't mean that you have to treat them like dirt. Stop being so hard on other people. Who are you to condemn them anyway? They need help just like you.

First of all, what does it mean to have no restraints? That means that your activity goes beyond what is socially or morally acceptable. That means that you go beyond what is good for your health or well being. In other words, it is more than enough so watch it. Neither of us need any excess baggage so watch it. What are you saying? I'm saying that you don't need any baggage that is heavier than the amount a passenger is allowed to take on a flight without an extra charge. Believe me somebody is going to be taxed or pay a little extra for bringing extra baggage, especially in a relationship, so watch it. Now this relationship could be with your parents, children, friend, spouse, business partner, etc. Whatever the relationship is that is putting the weight on you, you have to watch it and begin to lose all the excess weight before it becomes too addictive and you get too fat! It is going to take a lot of watching and praying to reach your goal or destiny.

> *Micah 6: 10-11*
> *Are there yet the treasures of wickedness*
> *in the house of the wicked, and the scant*
> *measure that is abominable? (verse 10)*
>
> *Shall I count them pure with the wicked*
> *balances, and with the bag of deceitful*
> *weights? (verse 11)*

What is going on in your house? How wicked is it? Are you that desperate that you have to store up stolen treasures and use dishonest measures of weight? You have gone to scant measures and that is abominable. Abominable meaning that this is extremely repugnant or offensive to God. Scant meaning that your weight is not sufficient. It is an inadequate amount for you to deal with. Can you count your house pure with the bag of dishonest weights? Stop trying to hide all those honeybuns. Who is that man that is staying or living with you right now, that is not your husband? It doesn't matter if he used to be your husband. It doesn't matter if you are soon to be married to him. It doesn't matter if it is your baby's daddy. Can you count your house pure with the bag of dishonest weights? No! Not with all that action going on!

Lets talk about the conversation at the well. You will find this in the book of John the fourth chapter beginning with the seventh verse. Why is it that the woman at the well had been in relationship after relationship? She had been married five times and she was still not satisfied. By this time she had given up on marriage I suppose. Jesus asked her to go and get her husband and come back. The woman at the well confessed her sin by saying, "I have no husband." I believe that even though the man she claimed was not her husband, was actually acting as her husband because she was probably sleeping with him and possibly living with him also. She had gone through five husbands.

Jesus revealed to her that He knew that. He told her, you had five husbands and the man you are with right now is not your husband. How many honeybuns have you had? How much weight have you gained. Marriage is sacred to God and sin is known unto God. Now as long as the woman continue to drink from the water that she chooses she will thirst again. Why? It is because she is choosing the same type of man. Jesus told her if she drink from the water that He would give her, then she would be satisfied. Her thirst will be satisfied. She will never thirst again. The water that Jesus will provide is the living water. There is nothing dead about it. God wants her to live a godly life. God wants her to do it His way. Her will needs to line up with Gods will. That's why it is so important to include God in your choosing because God will search the heart. As long as you continue to choose with your flesh then you will never be satisfied. We must do inventory on ourselves to find out why we keep getting in the wrong relationships. Have you noticed that you seem to be the common denominator in each relationship? My God after five husbands you should have learned to lean totally on God because your own choosing has been messed up lately.

I believe the woman at the well kept choosing the same type of man over and over again. They may look different but they are the same type. Why do you keep choosing people who are all about game? If you keep choosing this type of man then you will continue to thirst. Have you ever drunk anything that never quite quenched your thirst? It wasn't until you got some good refreshing water that actually quenched the thirst. What are you drinking and what are you thirsting for? What's really going on in your house?

What house are we speaking of anyway? Well the house could be the church house. The house could be your dwelling place. The house could be your personal temple. If you allow too much weight to be put on you then you won't be able to move when God say move. If you allow too much junk to be put in your house then your house will become cluttered along with your mind. So when it is time to move then all the junk that you have in your house will slow you down and clog up your ears. If you are not carrying the appropriate weight that is needed then you won't be able to move when God say move. You won't be able to run when God says run. You will be sluggish and tired because it will sap your strength. You will be slow to react or respond to God. You will lack alertness and energy. You will become so weary that you will be on the verge of giving up. Don't give up!

When you get to the point of giving up then you will begin to compromise and let anything go. People will walk all over you and treat you any kind of way with disrespect. Some relationships are not meant to be because of the weight it carries. Some relationships do not fit where you are going. That's why Colossians 3:18 reads, "Wives, submit yourselves unto your own husbands, as it is fit in the Lord." Fit means suitable and acceptable. That is why you don't submit to everything that the head does because it may not be suitable or acceptable to God. Now I know that this is messing some of you up but it is true. You can get caught up if you want to. If my head is trying to lead me to a bridge and he tells me to jump, I am not going to do it! I refuse to submit to something like that. Somebody better wake up! I know that is not fitting to God. I know that this is not acceptable to God! I am not the one! I have been a fool long enough when I called myself submitting to my head that was leading me to destruction. The enemy had me in sleep mode. I am sick and tired of sleeping with the enemy! God had to enlighten me and wake me up! Talk to God about your situation and He will lead and guide you in the right direction.

The bible says to acknowledge God in all thy ways and He will direct your path. You must have taken a wrong turn somewhere. But as long as you are filled with the Holy Ghost, there is hope. Are you filled with the Holy Ghost? Is your head filled with the Holy Ghost? Don't be fooled now. People may say some holy things but that does not mean that they have the Holy Ghost. They could have a form of godliness but denying the power thereof which causes them to be separated from the power. In order to have power you need the Holy Ghost.

> *But ye shall receive power, after that*
> *the Holy Ghost is come upon you.*
> *Acts 1: 8*

As long as you are filled with the Holy Ghost you shall be able to receive deliverance, healing, peace, wisdom, miracles, etc. That is receiving power. Listen, you don't have to speak in unknown tongues to have the Holy Ghost but it doesn't mean that you won't receive it. Some people have the Holy Ghost but have not been filled to the point of overflowing. And just because you have the gift of speaking in unknown tongues, does not make you better or more spiritual than the next person. Why do you say that? I say that because the devil has tongues also. Honey, you can speak in tongues and continue to shack up with someone that is not your husband. You can speak in tongues and cuss somebody out. You can speak in tongues and be sleeping with Tom, Dick and Harry. What are you talking about?

The Holy Spirit is a teacher. When the Holy Ghost has come upon you then you will become aware of stuff that's been there all the time. The Holy Ghost is your receiver. After you receive the Holy Ghost then you will began to pick up all kinds of signs and wonders when you finally tune in to the right channels. It was there all the time but you just didn't have your receiver, which is the Holy Ghost. You will began to see stuff you have been overlooking. Maybe you used to be on fire for the Lord, but now you have gotten so lazy and negative. Maybe you lost your fire and vision. God will give you new vision. God can do supernatural things in your life. All you have to do is call on Him and be sincere about it.

> *Hebrews 12: 1-2a*
> *Wherefore seeing we also are compassed*
> *about with so great a cloud of witnesses,*
> *let us lay aside every weight, and the sin*
> *which doth so easily beset us, and let us*
> *run with patience the race that is set before*
> *us. (verse 1)*
>
> *Looking unto Jesus the author and finisher*
> *of our faith. (verse 2a)*

You must lay aside every hindrance. You must lay aside every weight that is destroying you. You must forsake, abandon and withdraw from sin and run. So if an extremely fine good-looking married man come after you then you should run. If a fine good-looking single man come after you and you know you are not ready yet, then you should run. You must lay aside every hindrance and every weight. Did you hear that? Lay aside EVERY hindrance and EVERY weight. Run with patience. Keep hope alive and know that your time is coming but you must be patient. You need to have perseverance, which is determination because God has a plan for your life. Look at Christ's example because Christ is our inspiring example. Remember Jesus is the author, he wrote the book. Remember He is also the finisher of our faith. It's not over until God says it is over. When God says it is over then the weight is over. When God says it is over then you don't have to wait anymore because the wait is over.

You must spend time observing or watching something or someone closely especially in a relationship. You must listen for the weather alerts. You must be slow to speak and swift to listen. You need to know when a storm or a tornado is headed your way. Be alert and keep a good lookout for something that might appear or happen. When you watch you must be awake and not asleep. The reason is because you cannot observe anyone or anything if you are asleep. Open your eyes and get past the fine man. What is he really like after the infatuation? Wake up to see. Your eyes could be open but you could be blind as a bat. (Slang for blurred vision or cannot see) If you are not watchful, a baseball bat could be headed for you to bust you upside your head as if they were playing baseball. Now I don't know about you but I wouldn't want to submit to a head like that.

A watcher is somebody who acts as a guard or guardian. You should and must guard your heart and mind. That means to protect it through Christ Jesus. Let God be your personal guard because He never sleeps nor slumbers. He is always on duty. Observe and watch people when they are by themselves versus when they are with a group of people. For instance, when they are by themselves with you they may treat you extremely nice. On the other hand, if they are with a group of people around you, they may treat you with disrespect. I have had that happen to me several times. Observe and watch yourself also to the ways that you respond to the situation. Keep a lookout for something that might appear or happen. Become a person that stays awake spiritually and become a watcher of yourself also.

> *He hath said, which heard the words of*
> *God, and knew the knowledge of the most*
> *High, which saw the vision of the Almighty,*
> *falling into a trance, but having his eyes*
> *open. Numbers 24: 16*

God will give you spiritual knowledge and spiritual vision as long as you keep your eyes open and seek His face. God will give you spiritual knowledge and spiritual vision as long as you continue to seek Him diligently. You will be able to hear from God as long as you stay in His word and pray without ceasing. Be careful not to fall into a trance from evil influence. Don't let anyone put you into a dazed state.

You need to be aware of the environment that you are in so that you will be able to respond appropriately. The enemy will love to have you in a hypnotic state of mind. All it does is open doors for the enemy to enter. Keep your eyes open so that you can hear from God. You need spiritual knowledge and spiritual vision. You also need to be able to hear. Watch and pray. A watcher is somebody who acts as a guard or guardian. It is somebody who keeps a vigil. A vigil is a night watcher. It is a period spent in doing something through the night. It is a period of watching, guarding and praying. Watch out for tornadoes. Be alert! Join weight watchers today! Weight watchers are the smart ones!

Chapter 3
MISERY

What is misery? Misery simply means to suffer. Why do Christians suffer? Why are Christians so unhappy? What makes them miserable? Is it possible that we allowed ourselves to let somebody take us there? Lets look at the definition of misery. 1) It is the source of great unhappiness. It is something or someone that causes great unhappiness. 2) It is poverty. 3) It is anxiety, which is an agitated state of mind produced by real or imaginary fears.

What or who can cause you to have great unhappiness? What or who can cause you to live in poverty? What or who can agitate your mind to produce real or imaginary fears? The answer is no one other than the enemy. Remember when we said that people are not the enemy? We also said that people could be greatly influenced by the enemy. Now let me help you. Read this very carefully.

> *Galatians 6: 7-8*
> *Be not deceived: God is not mocked for whatsoever a man soweth, that shall he also reap. (verse 7)*
>
> *For he that soweth to his flesh shall of the flesh reap corruption, but he that soweth to the Spirit reap life everlasting. (verse 8)*

Let me help you with something here. This is Gods rule. This is a principle that God has set down. What a man sows, that is what he reaps. That's something to really think about.

This is a very important principle. This is something that we should definitely take note of as we live our daily lives. This is not something that you can forget about nor should you take it lightly. The principle is real. Therefore we better be careful what we do or say. We better be careful what we sow because whatever we sow, we will reap.

Now the scripture begins by saying: Warning! Be not deceived. The word deceived literally means to be led astray. It means to mislead somebody or hide the truth deliberately. It means to convince you of something that is not true. It is a dishonest practice. It is simply a trick of the enemy. The world is filled with people who have been deceived. People that think that the lie is the truth and the truth is a lie. Some people are deceived into thinking that Gods word is a lie. They don't know what to believe because they are confused. The enemy wants to keep you confused because he is the author of confusion. The enemy wrote the book on confusion. So if you are not clear and you are confused about something then look towards the enemy. If you are blind, then look towards the enemy.

Some people follow the enemy instead of the truth, because he has deceived them into thinking that his word is truth, rather than Gods word being truth. The enemy has been deceiving since the beginning of time. When the enemy first came into the Garden of Eden, he tricked Eve. He deceived her so that she thought that his word was the truth, rather than the word of God. So if you follow the enemy rather than God, then the enemy will lead you astray. Remember the truth leads you into godly living. The lie leads you into wicked living. If you choose to live a godly life then you must know and love the truth because the truth will make you free.

The enemy and even false teachers would like us to think that we can do anything and not reap the consequences of those things that we do or say. The devil is a liar! The enemy would like for us to think that we can do evil and reap well and good instead of evil. The devil is a liar! The enemy thinks that we can break Gods commandments and still be blessed. Be not deceived, God is not mocked.

To be miserable means to be in the state of suffering brought about by affliction. If you are miserable, then you are experiencing a serious lack of contentment. If you are miserable then you are living in discomfort and unpleasantness and this is a low down dirty shame. Lets look at the root word of misery or miserable. The root word is miser. What is a miser? A miser is an ungenerous or selfish person. It is someone who is mean and ungenerous. They are selfish and greedy. Not only does a miser hoard money but they literally hate spending their own. If you are not careful, they may even hoard you. As a result, though they may be rich physically, they tend to live their lives as if they were poor. They have a poverty mentality. In their heart they don't believe in tithing. When they do put money in church, it is to impress and not to be blessed.

Let me help you with something. They don't mind spending your money at all, but when it comes to them spending a little money, they get a little funny. What's wrong with that picture? I don't know if you know this or not, but being stingy is a curse. So if the bible states that you reap what you sow and you are always trying to reap where you haven't sown, then that can cause a problem. This situation itself can cause you to be miserable. For example, in a marriage you should sow tender loving care. If you tend to want to reap the tender loving care without sowing it, then you just might come up short! And let everybody say, Amen.

Chapter 4
MY STORY (Part I)

During this particular time in my life, I was in the home with my spouse. We were trying to make the best of something that wasn't meant to be. We were living in two different worlds. I was trying to love my God with all my heart, but my spouse was trying to love the world with all his heart. Of course there was a lot of satanic influence. My spouse was not the enemy and I knew that. But at the time he seemed to be. Let me remind you that the only marriage God ordains or joins together are two whole people filled with love and respect for one another. You both must be saved and filled with the Holy Spirit. Can this person meet you in the spirit? Will this person respect you? Are you equally yoked or is this a joke? Is this person equipped with the necessary ingredients to love you the right way? Will this person encourage you and build you up? If your marriage is a joke and you are living in misery, then maybe you chose with your flesh. I know I chose with my flesh and that's not funny at all. This is not a joke. This is not to be taken lightly. If you chose with your flesh then that means that this was a choice by man and not God.

Either you failed to get godly wisdom or you just didn't take heed to the warning signs. So if this is you, then you know the old saying, "You made your bed, now you got to sleep in it." Somebody lied to me. How long will you continue to sleep in a bed that is making you miserable. I was not free so I knew that this couldn't be God. I was missing some truth from the word of God. I must search the scriptures to find some answers. Let me tell you something. There is nothing nice about sleeping in a bed that is ruled by satanic influences. When I realized what and who was sleeping in my bed, I then said, "Lord, I got to stop sleeping with the enemy." I realized that I was being violated. The enemy was influencing my spouse to abuse his authority. After all, he was the head you know. No wonder I saw so much hatred. I know without a shadow of a doubt that the enemy does not like me. The enemy does not like what I stand for. No wonder it seemed like he was out to get revenge. If I continue to sleep with him, no doubt he would have murdered me even though I seemed to be dying anyway. The reason I say that is because my husband was employed by a satanic power. Listen ladies, this man whom I chose to make a covenant with was my head. But remember what God said in I Corinthians.

> *But I would have you know, that the*
> *head of every man is Christ, and the*
> *head of Christ is God.*
> *I Corinthians 11:3*

So what happens when Christ is not the head of your husband? Let me tell you what happens. If Christ is not leading your husband, then you will be headed for destruction. So it would be very wise to hear from God before you choose. Some way and some how you need to break the powers and the authority of the enemy. If you don't then you will die. You don't want that to happen to you now do you? This is a very serious thing. This is nothing to play with or to be taken lightly. You could actually die!

So why not be victorious and kill the relationship that is already dead and cut the head off the giant like David did and run. If you don't then the giant will make fun of you. The giant will curse you because of the demonic gods. I know you don't want to be cursed with a curse. I don't know about you but I don't want to stay in a house that has a curse on it. The giants' plan is to tear and rip you apart and feed you to the wild animals. The giant will actually insult your God. I mean they will do it without any fear. You must fight to live in the name of the Lord. The Lord will help you defeat the giant if you let Him. If you are a child of the king then you will win. I say that because the Lord wins all his battles. You just have to crack the skull of the giant like David did. If you are being attacked in the home, then you need to know that you can kill the giant without trying to preach or force the bible on him. Most likely they are not trying to hear it anyway.

> *Therefore David ran, and stood upon the Philistine, and took his sword, and drew it out of the sheath thereof, and slew him, and cut off his head therewith. And when the Philistines saw their champion was dead, they fled. I Samuel 17:51*

David was victorious because he put an end to the wicked. While everybody else was living in fear and letting the enemy do whatever he wanted to do, David decided to take a stand. He feared not because he knew that God was with him. I thought I was ready for marriage this time around but I was very wrong. Nobody could tell me that I didn't hear from God because I had my mind made up already to go through the marriage. Listen, a man is not equipped to love you the right way if he is not saved and filled with the Holy Spirit. It doesn't matter how nice he is from the beginning. I don't care how much he reads his bible in the beginning. I don't care how much he goes to church in the beginning. I don't care how much he prays in the beginning. All that can stop! If he is not a true man of God and his heart is not right, then he cannot and will not love you the right way.

It doesn't matter how much you pray either! Come on somebody, is this man whole? Is he a God fearing man? Is he filled with the Holy Ghost? Listen, there was a lot of hatred shown towards me in this marriage because of all the satanic influences. Before I got married, my spouse showed me that he was very interested in going to church. He showed me that he was very interested in reading the bible. He showed me that he was very interested in praying. He literally showed me that he was very interested in all three of these things until the honeymoon was over. It was all a trick to get in. Everything seemed to be good on the outside, but yet messed up on the inside. When his brother came to pick us up from the airport, we were waiting on our luggage, then his brother said, "You tricked her didn't you?" My spouse said with a little chuckle, "Yehhhh." I couldn't help but to wonder is he serious. Do I really know the man I married?

Listen, I know that I told you over and over again that he was not the enemy but one thing I do know is that the enemy took residence in his life and he allowed it continuously. The enemy built a big huge mess of a house. His temple was not clean but it was wicked. Now I am not saying that God didn't love him as much as he love me, but lets face reality. He showed me many signs of being a child of the devil (the enemy). It was very satanic. My mind became agitated. I am telling you the truth. We must pull the covers off the enemy. I was in an agitated state of mind with real fears. I began to question God. "God, am I in the wrong marriage?" "Did I choose with my flesh?" "Why did I get married?" "Why am I experiencing so much mess?" "Did I really hear from you

God?" "Did you really want me to stay single in spite of my loneliness?" "Tell me why am I experiencing so much pain in my marriage?" "Why all this abuse?" "Why do believers or Christians suffer?" "Why is there so much misery?"

Do you remember that we said misery means to suffer? Well suffer means to allow. We allow ourselves to go through all that pain. We do it to ourselves people! We make ourselves very unhappy because of our many choices. Don't get mad or angry with the Pastor, nor your family and friends. It's your fault! You should have listened to your Pastor when he tried to tell you in the first place. I remember when I didn't listen to my Pastor. Before I even entered this marriage, the Pastor tried to tell me that I wasn't ready for this one. He tried to tell me that this is not the right time. He even tried to tell me that he wasn't right for me. Oh but No! I wouldn't listen! I rebelled and found every excuse in the book to go through the marriage. We both actually said that if the Pastor would not have married us then we will go to the courthouse to get married. That is exactly what we did. We got married at the courthouse. Help us Lord, in Jesus name.

Now you know you had to miss God if you are lacking or in a state of extreme poverty. What I mean by that is that you become spiritually drained because of a marriage like this. You can become spiritually drained because of the head that is ruling the house. You may begin to compromise because of a marriage or house like this. Do not compromise! You do not want to be in a state of extreme poverty spiritually or naturally. Why? The reason is because poverty is a curse. There comes a time while you are yet suffering time and time again that you would want to put an end to all this. When your mind becomes extremely agitated then after so long you would want to put an end to all this. Now since we are all different then we will all deal with this type of situation differently.

I was at a point where I knew that I couldn't take it anymore. Not only was I sick of him but I was sick of myself! There is only so much a person can take before they actually take action one way or another. I got tired of all the pain and suffering. I got tired of all the abuse. I got tired of all the lies and cheating. I got tired of all the name-calling and all the putting down. This was even done in front of his children. I got tired of him calling me fat. Do you know what I mean? This man was a whole lot bigger than I was, but yet he continued to call me fat. As a matter of fact you probably would have looked at his belly and thought he was carrying triplets but yet he continued to call me fat. That is not building up or encouraging, but it is tearing down one another.

All my children were grown but not pleased with my choice, but yet they respected my decision. My own spouse even called my child out of his name several times. The first time he did it, I told him don't you ever do that again. I told him, I have never and will never call any of your children out of their names. Guess what? It continued anyway. This particular child was very quiet and minded his own business. This was also the same child of mine that had been in and out of the hospitals quite a bit. He has already been through enough. So why would he do such a thing? By this time I was beginning to allow the enemy to influence me greatly. I now realize that the attacks were so heavy because of the call on my life. If the enemy can't affect you then he will try to affect you through your children. You must be very careful not to put your children in danger also. Lets face facts. I was dealing with an evil devil. My spouse did not want the presence of God but he just wanted the position of being head.

How many of you true mothers will admit that we get very agitated when it comes to our children? I'm talking about the true mothers. I am not talking about the mothers who will leave their babies behind all because of a man. I am not talking about the mothers who will turn their back on their own children to be with a man. I am not talking about the mothers who try to justify what they are doing is right even though they left their children behind. I am talking about the real mothers who will train their children in the way they should go as the bible states. These mothers will train their children whether a real father is absent or not and whether a real father wants to train them or not. There are some men that can be a real father or better father to your children than any biological father would ever be!

Don't mess with my baby! I was losing vision because I was beginning to take my eyes off of God. Now according to him, his children did no wrong, but my children he showed inconsistent respect. Sometimes they are okay but other times he's putting them down. I couldn't agree with a lot of his parenting skills. There was nothing godly about it. What was I thinking to go through this marriage? He wanted to do it the world's way, while I'm trying to do it Gods way. For example, he did not like his youngest son's honesty. He was teaching him to be a liar. He was also teaching him to be a player. It was more important for him to be a player than to get his schoolwork. He told him you must have more than one girlfriend at the age of about thirteen. When the different girls began to call in the middle of the night, he was a proud daddy. Even though he had to get up for school the next day, he wasn't concerned about him getting his proper sleep. That was a shame to see the baby in sleep mode also. He was following his daddy's instruction. After all he was his head and little did he know his daddy was putting him to sleep. I prayed heavily for him to wake up out of sleep. We must be careful whom we choose to lead and guide our children. This is so important. We must wake up and wake our children up also. We must stop sleeping with the enemy.

I can now understand the reasons why he would fail in school or couldn't stay focused. His own son said that his daddy, at the time, didn't know how to discipline him or teach him the right way. He said that I was the best mother he had ever had. He wanted to do right but he had an evil force watching over him. My children today still call him their brother. Now here I am an evangelist living in all this mess. I was living in hell. What am I to do? Listen, God knows your good works and tribulation and poverty that you face, but you are rich in God. God also knows the fake people who profess they are of God, but yet they are the children of the devil (the enemy). They have a form of godliness but they deny the power thereof.

> *Revelation 2:9-10a*
> *I know thy works, and tribulation, and poverty, (but thou art rich) and I know the blasphemy of them which say they are Jews, and are not, but are the synagogue of Satan. (verse 9)*
>
> *Fear none of those things which thou shalt suffer: behold, the devil shall cast some of you into prison, that you may be tried; (verse 10a)*

Truly I was tried. The enemy did cast me into prison in my own home. I was hurt and I was living in hell in my own home. I would go to church and smile with no one even knowing what I was experiencing at home. Then I would leave church, go home only to feel locked up in hell again. After ministering, sometimes I would go home and get in battles of literally cussing one another out. That is what the enemy wanted, but I knew somehow, I had to get out of this situation. I thought I was past all of the profanity, but I found out it was still in me. I didn't want to cuss him out, but I did it anyway. I hadn't used profanity in so long that I thought I had forgot how. Well it didn't take long to get it back with the bad choices I made. Can I just keep it real? It felt good to my flesh when I did it. I called myself giving him a piece of his own medicine and a piece of my mind.

I wondered to myself, if I would ever escape before something terrible would happen. I was cheated out of my peace because the wicked knows no peace. I was cheated out of my peace because of his twisted way of thinking. My life was in turmoil. The rules were broken. Even though God said, "Be not deceived," I was deceived. My spouse was misleading. He was untrue to his duties as a godly husband. He was untrue to our beliefs in God and His will. He was just simply unfaithful and untrue. I was cheated out of the better things in life. Even though I realize now that I was wrong in choosing this marriage, I asked God, "Could you please give me back my peace?"

Chapter 5
CHEATERS

Definition of cheaters:

1. To deceive somebody (to deceive or mislead somebody, especially for personal gain).
2. Break rules to gain advantage (to break rules in attempt to gain an unfair advantage).
3. Be unfaithful to somebody (untrue to commitments, duties, beliefs, or ideals. To have sexual relationship with somebody other than a spouse).

If you are a cheater, then that means that you are dishonest and untruthful. Cheaters can cause you to lose your strength and power. The kind of strength and power I am speaking of is physical and spiritual strength. There is dissipation (disappearance) of physical and spiritual strength by iniquity. There are ways to lose your physical and spiritual strength by iniquity.

> *Psalms 31:9-18*
> *Have mercy upon me, O Lord, for I am*
> *in trouble: mine eye is consumed with*
> *grief, yea, my soul and my belly.*
> *(verse 9)*

In other words, Lord I need help. I am hurting and can hardly see through this mess that it seem I'm almost blind. My whole body aches. This is deep Lord! What am I to do concerning this marriage?

For my life is spent with grief, and my
years with sighing: my strength faileth
because of mine iniquity, and my bones
are consumed. Psalms 31:10

God, I have known only sorrow all of my marriage long. And I suffer month after month and year after year. My strength is failing because of the iniquity I face. I am weak from sin and my bones are limp. I have been used up down to the bone. I don't even know if I could ever recover from this.

I was a reproach among all mine enemies,
but especially among my neighbors, and
a fear to mine acquaintance: they that did
see me without fled from me. Psalms 31:11

God, the people who are my enemies insult me. Neighbors are even worse. I disgust my family and friends because of all the talk against me. People meet me on the streets and they turn and run away just to avoid me. I was blamed for what was happening in my marriage and discredited. I suffered.

I am forgotten as a dead man out of mind:
I am like a broken vessel. Psalms 31:12

God, my husband completely forgot me. He neglected me. He left me behind and did not remember me. I am broken God. I have been broken all into pieces like a broken dish. I was broken which means that I was no longer whole. I was no longer in working condition. I was not honored. I was not respected or fulfilled by my husband. There were so many broken promises. We were uneven. I was physically weak. I was being destroyed by adversity. We were split apart by divorce (without the divorce decree). We were split apart by separation. We were split apart by desertion while we were yet still legally married and living together as husband and wife. God I was incomplete. I was lacking parts necessary to complete me. The whole household was disorganized. We were lacking order and harmony. I was merely a broken vessel or broken dish that was being thrown away. In the mean time and in between time, I learned a valuable lesson about being broken. After going through all that I've been through, I have been broken from saying to myself or anybody else that I must have a man in my life at all times. This has taught me how to wait on the Lord. I am no longer anxious.

> *For I have heard the slander of many: fear*
> *was on every side: while they took counsel*
> *together against me, they devised to take*
> *away my life. Psalms 31:13*

In other words, God, people were making false and malicious statements about me that could have damaged my reputation. I regretted this, but it also frightened me. They were plotting and scheming against me along with my husband. This was taking the life out of me because he was making false malicious statements about me also.

> *But I trusted in thee, O Lord: I said, Thou*
> *art my God. Psalms 31:14*

> *My times are in thy hand: deliver me*
> *from the hand of mine enemies, and*
> *from them that persecute me.*
> *Psalms 31:15*

> *Make thy face to shine upon thy servant;*
> *save me for thy mercies sake. Psalms 31:16*

In other words, God, even though I was getting weak to all the disappointments, I continued to put my trust in you Lord. I claim you as my God. My life is in your hands. Save me from enemies who hunt me down. Rescue me from them that harass or victimize me. Deliver me from those who persecute me. Deliver me from those who afflict, oppress and torment me. Smile on me, your servant. I want to know what it means to have joy again. I want to be able to smile again. Have sympathy and rescue me.

> *Let me not be ashamed, O Lord; for I have*
> *called upon thee: let the wicked be*
> *ashamed, and let them be silent in the grave.*
> *Psalms 31:17*

> *Let the lying lips be put to silence; which*
> *speak grievous things proudly and*
> *contemptuously against the righteous.*
> *Psalms 31:18*

In other words, I pray only to you, Lord God. Please don't disappoint me. I have been through plenty of disappointments. Now disappoint my cruel enemies until they lie silent in their graves since they are already dead. They should be embarrassed or regretful for treating anybody so badly. Disappoint my cruel enemies until the destruction or end of this mess is silenced. Silence them like the "k" in knight. This is not my knight and shining armor. This type of man cannot protect me nor be devoted to me and yet he is full of darkness. He might as well ride that horse in another direction. Silence those super proud liars! Make them stop bragging and insulting your people.

Since this was taking the life out of me, I was continuously getting weaker each and everyday. I was losing strength. I was at a point where I couldn't take the abuse anymore. At this point, I no longer looked at my husband as my husband anymore. I began to look at him as the enemy. The enemy was really putting many thoughts in my mind of what to do. I was in many ways like the woman with the issue of blood. We all know that we have to deal with the issues of life.

In the passage of scriptures, Luke 8:43-48, the woman had an issue that lasted for years. I can imagine she was thinking enough is enough. I can relate because I have had enough. This issue has been going on far too long and I just can't seem to get the medicine that I need. It seemed to be no hope because the medicine I was taking and the food that I allowed to be served on my plate was making me worse and not better. This issue was lasting too long. That means that she needed to get out of that situation and do it now. Listen, I knew that I needed to come out of this situation because the pain was so...ooo...ooo Great! Tony the tiger doesn't have anything on this one. I almost had a nervous breakdown. Sorry devil, its not happening! You picked the wrong one baby!

So since I had reached my peak, anything he would have said out of the way, could have made me snap, crackle and pop. (Slang for handle the situation) I no longer looked at the spirit or the enemy that was influencing him, but I began to look at him in the flesh realm. I no longer wanted to fight spiritually, but I wanted to fight physically (carnally or fleshly). I wanted to result back to my past of fighting physically. That is how I used to solve any situation that bothered me in the past, by taking it to blows. I said to myself, you want to go there, then lets go there. I was beginning to sink like Peter when he took his eyes off of God after dealing with a storm. So one day, I cried out to God like I normally do especially when I have messed up. I wanted to know what to do about this situation.

I needed a touch from Jesus to strengthen me. At this time if I couldn't get a touch from Jesus, then I just might have to touch my husband myself. That wouldn't be anything nice. I said, "God, I can't take this anymore." I had people on the outside, trying to look on the inside of my circumstances, not knowing my pain. Yet they were telling me to stay together. In spite of that, I knew that I needed a way out, even though I was trying to remain standing.

> *I Corinthians 10:12-13*
> *Wherefore, let him that thinketh he*
> *standeth take heed lest he fall.*
> *(verse 12)*
>
> *There hath no temptation taken you but*
> *such as is common to man: but God is*
> *faithful, who will not suffer (allow) you*
> *to be tempted above that ye are able;*
> *but will with the temptation also make*
> *a way to escape, that ye may be able to*
> *bear it. (verse 13)*

Even if you think you can stand up to temptation, be careful not to fall. We are tempted in the same way everyone else is tempted. This is nothing new. It is common to man. You need to know that God can be trusted not to let you be tempted too much and He will show you how to escape (to flee) from your temptation. What does it mean to escape? Escape means 1) to break free from captivity. 2) to avoid a bad situation. 3) a means of getting away. 4) to avoid danger, harm, or involvement in an unpleasant situation. If you do not escape then you can turn into a plant that spreads from a beautiful garden but is now growing wild.

When I first approached him about going to a marriage counselor he said, "I don't need it but you need it." Eventually he gave in. We went to a spiritual marriage counselor but that didn't help. He even had them fooled because of his charm. Later they found out differently about him and it shocked them. He literally tried to run a game on them also. Tell me something. What makes anyone think that counseling will help when you are dealing with a devil? You don't counsel a devil but you cast him out! Wake up!

Chapter 6
MY STORY (Part II)

One Sunday morning while watching Christian TV, God was giving me an answer on what to do through one of my spiritual daddies. It was time to escape! Psalm 112:4 states the light can rise in darkness. The wisdom came. This is what God said to me.

> *I want you to live and not die. He that*
> *flees today can live to preach tomorrow.*
> *Because of tradition, some Christians*
> *think that you are supposed to suffer.*
> *(allow things to happen to you). He said,*
> *your dying is not going to save the world,*
> *but Jesus dying helped save the world.*
> *He said, if you die, you will be no good*
> *for the Kingdom.*

Listen my sisters, I was getting weaker and weaker each day almost reaching death. Now I had no idea of what was going to happen after I received this word, but God did. Sometimes God will allow you to go through trauma to show how great He is. He may allow you to go through the fire knowing He is the controlling factor of how hot it gets. My God can turn the heat up or He can turn the heat down. How many of you know that God is all knowing and He is in control? Let me remind you that my spouse and I were not communicating very well. It seemed that many times that I wanted to talk with him or wanted to address an issue, he wasn't interested. He was rebellious and very passive. So now that I am receiving a word from God this Sunday morning on Christian TV, guess what? He was now ready to talk. I knew that this message was specifically for me.

I was getting instruction on what to do. So when he asked me to talk then I knew immediately that the enemy did not want me to receive this word. I told him I am sorry I cannot talk with you right now because God is giving me a great word. Now right there, I can hear somebody in the spirit missing that and saying, "You know that was wrong, she should have stopped whatever she was doing to sit and talk with her husband." You know when you face issues, people tend to judge you. How dare you judge me! You don't know what I've been through to get here. I was desperate for a word from God. The fact that I survived this relationship is a miracle in itself. Listen, God is first in my life and plus my husband was blind, couldn't see and had no vision. Somebody better wake up!

So after the man of God was done ministering, I went directly to my husband to ask him what did he want to talk about. He was known for talking to me any kind of way, as I told you before in the previous chapters. So while he was laying across the couch in the living room, he began to talk down to me again. So I politely departed from the living room went back into my bedroom and pulled out the gun. Did she say gun? Yes I said gun! In my mind I was thinking, "Hello to my little friend." I was thinking that he has talked down to me for the last time and he will not live to put anyone else down. I thought I would be doing every female a favor. So after I pulled the gun out, I then laid it on the pillow at the edge of the bed where I was sitting. I looked at the gun while thinking of all the things I went through. I then got up, walked back down the hallway slowly with my hands behind my back. When I got to the entry of the living room, I asked him slowly, "Now what did you say to me?" Immediately he began to speak nice words to me. I'm sorry, but when I think of this time in my life it really makes me sad. It makes me sad because I know that what I was doing was not of God and I definitely wanted to please God.

I realized that it was the enemy that I was sleeping with in my mind that caused me to think that my spouse didn't deserve to live because of all the pain he put me through. He deserves to live just as much as I do. There is still hope for his deliverance today. It took me a while to be able to start praying for him again. Listen, you do not have to stay in an abusive relationship or marriage. Don't die, live! The enemy was telling me that he didn't deserve to live. I didn't think life belonged to him. We all know that the enemy will always put thoughts in our mind. The enemy wants to divide and conquer anyway. But there is nothing to divide if you go into a marriage divided. So if the marriage is already divided then the next thing for the enemy to divide is you from God.

Why should I kill someone physically who is already dead spiritually? I blame myself for making bad choices. I was trying to get something out of him that he didn't have to give. His cup was empty spiritually. He wasn't equipped to love me the right way. Like the woman with the issue of blood who had many worthless physicians. They couldn't help her and he couldn't help me. Just like my family and friends couldn't help me. The Pastor couldn't help me. Only Jesus could help me! This woman with the issue gave her all and it still got worse. She suffered. She suffered because she put her confidence in somebody who wasn't for her but against her. Listen, a person can form their mouth to tell you anything but that doesn't mean that it is true. Just because a person tells you that they love you doesn't mean that it is true. A person can tell you that they love you and show you hatred. That doesn't add up! That does not compute!

This woman suffered because she put her trust and confidence in someone who was full of trickery, deception, scheming and manipulation. But if God be for you, who can be against you? At this time in my life, I had lost all my peace because I was focusing on myself and how I felt. But the bible says in Isaiah 26:3, "God will keep you in perfect peace, if you keep your mind stayed on Him." We must trust in the Lord forever. For in the Lord Jehovah there is everlasting strength. We must trust God and keep our mind on Him. My mind at this point was on my spouse being the enemy. I no longer looked at him being influenced by the enemy, but I was looking at him as the enemy that slept in the same bed with me.

Now lets continue my story. When I asked him, "Now what did you say to me?" He immediately began to speak nice words to me, which came as a shock. I know now that it was God who stepped in. Trust me, God stepped in right on time. I needed that touch. Not only did he save my life but he saved my husbands life as well. That lets me know that God still loves us both in spite of the circumstances. Even though he was mean to me, there is still hope for him.

Neither one of us died physically from it because we are still here. After I was so shocked with the kind words that he said to me, all I could do was pause and then started to walk. I just walked backwards down the hallway with my hands behind my back to return to my bedroom. I then put the gun away. Thank you Jesus! I am forever in your debt! I really know the true meaning of being bought with a price now!

Listen, I had an infirmity that took me into this type of situation. An infirmity is a weakness of our human nature.

There are different kinds of infirmities. The first one that I will mention is sickness or disease. I am speaking of myself because I was burdened down with the sickness to have a man. I thought that my life could not be complete without a man in my life. That is a sickness in itself because you don't need a man to make you whole. If you choose to marry, make sure that your spouse is whole as well as yourself. Pray and fast so that you may be able to hear from God clearly. The second infirmity that I will mention is the imperfections of the body. I took the liberty of looking up the imperfections of man in one of my bible concordances. It stated that it is manifested in total corruption and it took me to the book of Isaiah.

> *Isaiah 1:5-6*
> *Why should ye be stricken any more?*
> *Ye will revolt more and more: the whole*
> *head is sick, and the whole heart faint.*
> *(verse 5)*

This scripture blew my mind when I read it. I had to ask myself the same questions. Why should I stay here and keep taking this punishment? Why not give up this sin? Revolt means to rebel against. It means that you will protest against the authority and their rules. I know that I protested and rebelled against the head because he was not being led by my God Almighty at all. It was nasty, unattractive and unpleasant to me. My head, which was my spouse, was sick and badly bruised which caused me to get sick. At that time I was feeling weak all over. I felt like I was about to fall out and faint. I needed a physician. Is there no balm in Gilead? My God, the health of your daughter needs to be recovered because I do not want a spiritual disease.

*From the sole of the foot even unto the
head there is no soundness in it, but
wounds, and bruises, and putrifying
sores: they have not been closed, neither
mollified with ointment. Isaiah 1: 6*

Listen to this. From the top of his head to the bottom of his feet, he was a mess. I even became a mess. The music that was playing and the noise he was talking sounded a mess. It was not healthy for him or myself at all. I was deprived from hearing the right sounds because of the bad influence and my bad choice. I needed to hear a sound from heaven so that I could remain healthy, be free from injury and be free from disease or illness. So be careful not to catch anything. Guard your anointing. Many times when you have been wounded, bruised and putrefied (having a foul smell) usually they will begin to stink very badly. Remember if your head stinks, then you will begin to stink if you are not careful. Don't you know that sores are painful and can become infected? Sores can cause great worry or distress especially open infected wounds. There are three remedies that the scripture gives you concerning this type of situation.

(1). Close the bruises or wounds. The act of closing causes you to move on or move something so that an opening or hole is covered or blocked. You might have to shut the business down. You may have to deactivate that file or program. You may have to terminate or bring that situation to an end. We are the determining factor in whether the devil (the enemy) can operate in our life or not. Ephesians 4:27 reads, "Neither give place to the devil." When we allow openings in our spiritual life then the devil feels he has the right to take residence. If we keep the doors closed he cannot do what he would like to do. Ignorance of the word of God can leave openings in our lives that are devastating. If you don't know your rights as a child of God then how can you defend yourself?

(2). Bind the enemy up. Stop him from stealing from you or spoiling your goods. The goods were fine until the enemy started hanging around your house. Matthew 12:29 reads, "Or else how can one enter into a strong man's house, and spoil his goods, except he first bind the strong man?" Not only can he spoil his house but he can spoil your house also. One stronghold can stop you from getting your stuff. Listen, it is Gods will for you to be free from every evil influence of the devil. He wants you to enjoy all the good things He has planned for your life. Don't let the enemy rob you of your goods anymore.

(3). Finally the scripture tells you to mollify with ointment. Mollify meaning that you can calm, soothe, or make something less intense or severe. You can make something less hard, rigid or stiff. How? I will tell you how, by using the oil of God. Say ointment take me away. Use this ointment or oil as if it was Calgon. Ointment is used on the skin to soothe soreness or itchiness, help wounds heal, or make the skin softer. Ointment is a salve made of olive oil and spices. Go ahead and spice your olive oil up with some anointing. You might need a little fasting and praying with your bottle. After you and the prayer warriors have prayed over it, then anoint yourself. The oil destroys the yoke that keeps people bound. Sin and sickness must depart when you recognize the oil of God. Go ahead and tell the enemy whatever you bring to me, you can't hold me. If you are struggling with diabetes, tell the devil, you can't hold me. If you are struggling with any trials, tell the devil, you can't hold me. Why? It is because sin and sickness must depart.

I realize that I am not perfect and that we all fall short of the glory of God. Hopefully you won't fall that short like I did. The last infirmity that I will mention is moral defects. I missed God because there was a defect in my principles of right conduct due to the bad choices I made. I had a personal flaw, a personal failing, weakness, or shortcoming, especially in my character. That's why it is so important to be filled with the Holy Spirit in order to deal with certain situations. When we pray, the Holy Spirit can intercede for us when we out of ignorance don't know what to pray for. We need our divine helper.

> *Likewise the Spirit also helpeth our*
> *infirmities: For we know not what we*
> *should pray for as we ought: but the*
> *Spirit itself maketh intercession for us*
> *with groanings which cannot be*
> *uttered. Romans 8:26*

Don't quench the Holy Spirit. Let the Holy Spirit do His work. Some of us are too busy trying to extinguish, put out, or leave out the Holy Spirit. Remember that the Holy Spirit is the third person of the triune God and it is within His personality to help our infirmities. Whatever you do please don't grieve the Spirit of God.

> *John 5:5-9*
> *And a certain man was there which had*
> *an infirmity thirty and eight years.*
> *(verse 5)*

63

How long have you had your infirmity? How long will you let your relationships cripple you? Thirty-eight days, thirty-eight months or thirty-eight years can be too long.

> *When Jesus saw him lie, and knew that*
> *he had been now a long time in that case*
> *he saith unto him, Wilt thou be made*
> *whole? John 5:6*

God knows who and what you are lying with. He knows what you are dealing with and He will show you some compassion because His vision is divine, but you must want help. If you don't want help then you need to know that God is a God of judgement also.

> *The impotent man answered him, Sir, I*
> *have no man, when the water is troubled,*
> *to put me into the pool: but while I am*
> *coming, another steppeth down before*
> *me. John 5:7*

My spouse couldn't help me and he was not my friend so I was helpless and friendless. To me I didn't have a man when the water was troubled. To me I didn't have a husband like the woman at the well said to Jesus. To me I was just sleeping with him. I had heard many messages about being married. I had heard that where you are weak your spouse would be strong enough to build you up. I heard that they would help lift you up or even encourage you to make it. I didn't have a man like that so to me I didn't have a man. While I was burning in hell at home, I needed some water to cool me off. I needed some cooling water because I was in trouble and the situation was getting hotter. I had to realize that he couldn't lead me or guide me to the pool because he was blind. He couldn't see the pool. He didn't even know there was a pool. He was too busy trying to step down on me and in front of me. I tell you today that I am not following anybody to a ditch.

> *Jesus saith unto him, Rise, take up*
> *thy bed, and walk. John 5:8*

You need to stand up and grow up so that you can gain a greater height or gain a greater level. You need to stand up and expect to increase, expect to achieve higher wealth, status, or importance. You need to stand up and increase your quality. Increase your values. Get you some respect! You may have been held back but the devil owes you. Tell the devil that you want a refund. You must gain possession of the things you lost or given up. Take back what the enemy stole from you. God will give you double for your trouble but stop sleeping in that bed and begin walking. Don't get caught up like I did. Don't let the enemy put you to sleep like he put me to sleep. Acknowledge God in all your ways and He will direct your path.

Get up! Dust yourself off! Shake the dust off your feet! Now move on! Move on, I say! When God says to kill something then anything that you won't kill will kill you. If you keep holding on to it when you know you should kill it then it will destroy you. Just put one foot in front of the other and move on! You got to move on so that God can give you divine direction but you have to make an effort to walk. An effort is demanded when it comes to this type of relationship. Each day that I began to wake up out of sleep, it caused me to become irritable or be in an angry mood right from the start of the day because of myself. I was not too happy with myself at the time. It was because of the bad choices I made. I was really upset with myself because I thought I had it together. I was angry with my spouse for allowing the enemy to influence him in a mighty way. I thought I heard from God and I wouldn't let anyone tell me otherwise. Please learn from my mistakes and don't do what I have done. Pray without ceasing!

> *And immediately the man was made*
> *whole, and took up his bed, and*
> *walked. John 5:9*

If that man can do it, then you can do it. If I can do it, then you can do it. When you are powerless, God will give you power. When you have an infirmity you can be healed and made whole again. Let God give you divine direction and move on! Rise, take up your bed and walk! When you really get tired of your situation, then you will say enough is enough! I got to go!

Chapter 7
WARNING!
SIGNS AND WONDERS

I am sure everybody knows what a warning sign is right? Well let's make sure that you have the correct understanding.

> *Wisdom is the principal thing;*
> *therefore get wisdom: and with all*
> *thy getting get understanding.*
> *Proverbs 4:7*

This is one way to get graded like you did when you were in school. In this scripture it reads, Wisdom is the principal thing. When you see the word principal, it is very important because he or she was the head of school in education or the head administrator. Since wisdom is the principal, then lets go back to school on this. Don't get in trouble with the principal by not choosing to abide by the rules. Why? It is because you may be sent to the office for discipline. So now we know that wisdom is very important since it is the principal thing. Wisdom is the head of schooling. Wisdom is the head administrator. Therefore it is time to get wisdom and with all thy getting get an understanding.

What is a warning? A warning can be a sign of something bad is coming. It could be a threat or a sign that something bad is going to happen. A warning can be advice to be careful or stop doing something. A warning could be telling you that you are taking a risk or that you are going in the wrong direction. A warning can tell somebody about something that might cause injury or harm. A warning could be telling you to be cautious. It could tell you do not enter into a place. Do you get the picture? Sometimes you need to take wise counsel or take advice. Lets look at the road signs for instance. Consider these signs before entering into a relationship. It could be a relationship before entering in a marriage. It could be a relationship before entering in a partnership in a business. It could be a relationship of becoming a member of a specific church. Look for signs. Seek God if you are in question. Watch for the signs. Signs can do wonders for you. Here are the road signs that you need to look for and obey them.

Stop Sign

A stop sign tells you to cease from moving. It tells you to come to a stand still. It means discontinue. Sometimes you need to stop before you even get started in a relationship. The reason I say that is because sometimes you think that you are ready to partner up with someone but yet you are not quite ready. For one thing you may not be whole yet. Just stand still and let God work on you because you or they may be under some construction. Let God transform you into wholeness first. Make sure before you say I do, that you and he are saved and filled with the Holy Ghost. Make sure that you are equally yoked and that's no joke. If after you have began the relationship anyway and you realize that it is all wrong, then you must cease from moving any further in the relationship before you get hurt.

Yield Sign

A yield sign tells you to slow down or stop in order to let another pass you by. Sometimes you need to yield or slow down and let someone you may choose to be in relationship with to start passing you by. The reason is because they may not fit you. They may not fit where you are going. Why? The reason is because there are some bad, bad boys out there. They may hinder you or even stop you from getting to your destiny. Find out before you decide to sign on the dotted line. If they don't fit with your lifestyle and you see a sign that demands you to yield, then don't force it. Slow down. You must look for values and quality.

Construction

A construction sign tells you that there is a process of building going on. It could be a large structure such as a house, road or bridge. You must also be aware of the materials that may be in the way of the building. Be aware of the type of quality or structure you are dealing with. Research if you must. Do you even know the man's last name? You must always be aware of the relationships you are involved in. The person could be under some heavy construction. If they are, then you could be the material that is in the way of the building. If you decide to go ahead and enter into a relationship with someone that is under construction, then this could cause you a lot of heartache and pain. Please don't do it! Check it out first!

Speed Limit

A speed limit sign tells you the maximum speed permitted, usually specified by law, at which a vehicle may travel on a particular stretch of road. Some people like to get into relationships and run away into the sunset. They run away with it. They shift in high gear to speed up the process when in fact they should go at a moderate speed. You fall in love so quickly, and it's too fast. You even get goose bumps when you see him. Shortly after that you start saying things like, "I love him and I'm going to marry him." Question. "Why do people turn their backs on their dearest spiritual friends after asking them their opinion?" Maybe they see what you don't see because of your knight blindness. There could be all kind of objects in the road that you don't see. You are too busy trying to ride into the sunset with your knight and shining armor that you have closed your ears to wise counsel. Tell me what are they working with on the inside, huh? Baby, don't you make a move too soon. Please look for signs, take your time and do the speed limit. Don't try to make your mind up or come to a conclusion so fast. Your speed should be moderate. You will be all right once you get over the goose bumps or the bumps in the road. Don't breakdown by hitting a pothole moving so fast. Don't get a ticket for speeding. It will cost you something. As a matter of fact, it could cost you too much.

Enter Sign

This traffic sign tells you that it is all right to go or come into a place. It tells you that it is all right to become a member of. It is all right to join or become officially involved in something. When you enter in something, you sign up for it. You become one of the parties bound by a contract. When you receive signs that clearly states that it is all right to enter into the relationship or marriage, then go ahead and sign on the dotted line. Remember you must be absolutely sure that you are hearing from God himself. The reason is because if you sign on the dotted line then whatever that person is carrying on the inside is coming also. If you choose wrongly then they could bind you or hinder you from your purpose in God. Hopefully you will join a whole man or woman of God with nothing missing and nothing broken. I have a question. Before you enter, are you absolutely sure that this man can love you like Christ loves the church? Let me talk to my brothers. Are you absolutely sure that this woman will love you enough to submit to you while God is leading you? You know some sisters give a lot of lip service. Did God give you the grace to deal with that if it occurs? Are you prepared to respect one another? Will you also serve, encourage and build one another up? If you believe that it is your time then go ahead and sign on the dotted line.

Do Not Enter Sign

This road sign tells you that it is not all right to go or come into a place. It is not all right to become a member. It is not all right to join or become officially involved in something. You are not to sign up for it anyway because you are not to enter into it. You are not to become one of the parties bound by a contract. If you enter into a relationship when the sign clearly states do not enter, then get ready for heartache and pain. Why would you choose to marry someone you have never seen before in your life. All you've seen is a fake picture on the Internet. How do you know that that person is who he says he is? All you've had is Internet conversation. You may seriously harm yourself for entering anyway after knowing this. Look at the signs. What are they telling you? Do not sign on the dotted line! Do not do it anyway! Do not listen to your flesh when it tells you that you are really thirsting after such a relationship. Do not act like you are starving for a man or a woman. Some of you just have to have attention. You are not to be the next victim bound by a contract. You want to be the victor that overcomes entering into bad relationships, especially dead ones. Be a person with integrity. Show your godly character. Let your light shine. Remember that light does not mix with darkness. Open your eyes very wide to see the signs. This is important!

Detour

A detour sign means to turn from a more direct or sure route or even a shorter route. If you enter in a relationship with someone who needs work or is being worked on, then you may have to go the long way around to reach your destiny. It could have been shorter. What will happen is, you will run right into a detour as long as you enter into a wrong relationship. A detour is a route to be taken by traffic as an alternative to the normal route when the normal route cannot be used. It is because you chose not to use it. Now that you have gotten off course by entering in a wrong relationship, then it is not possible to go the normal route because of your bad choice. Get ready to see all kinds of mess on the road. I am sure that the road will be a little rocky. Why did you change from your previously directed and expected way anyway? Are you getting too anxious? I thought your mind was made up. I thought you had the right course of action. Those of you that choose to take the detour and get off track can get back on track again. You must stay focused and look for the objects in the road. Help us Lord, in Jesus Name!

Highway Sign

Highway signs tell you the main road that you are on. It tells you the principal road you are traveling. Always look to God for signs. Look to the hills from which comes your help. All of our help comes from God. When you are traveling on the highway, let God tell you the main road you are on so that you can keep your focus of where you are headed. This could be very helpful to you. Let God reveal to you the principal road you are traveling. You need to know where you are headed. There is that word principal again. Remember when we said that when you see the word principal that means that this is very important. So in other words, it is very important to know what type of road you are traveling. Wisdom is very important. With all thy getting please get some understanding. It is very important to know where you are headed or where you are going. If you are not sure then ask God to reveal it to you. He is willing and able to do just that.

Exit Sign

An exit sign tells you the means of leaving a place. It is departure. It is an act of leaving a room, building or gathering. It is death or departure from life. It means you could die or cease to live. It means to go offstage or leave the stage during a performance of a play. There are so many people that are all about playing games with you. They will put on an act as if they have enrolled in a drama play just to get what they want from you. Don't get played, just exit. Depart or get off this road because it could take you to a place that you don't want to be. Please don't get caught up in the mix with light and darkness because you could die trying to stay there when it is time to exit! Listen when God gave me the exit sign, I called my mother and sister to let them know what I was doing. As I was packing my clothes in the car, they came over. They probably came over because I told them I didn't know what he might do next even though he was not there at the time. When he returned home, I was still packing my things in the car. My mother and sister got a chance to witness some of the disrespect that I was dealing with. He had even lied and disrespected my mother. Honey, If a man disrespects your mother and his own mother, then you know you got a problem on your hands. Even though God told me to exit before it got to this point, I knew for sure inside that it was my exit time! The longer I waited, the hotter it got in the household. Listen,

I had to break because I knew my break through was coming. I had to ask myself, "Why are you trying to be faithful to a dead thing?"

Now everyone have different reactions to warnings. Some of us obey the warning, some accept the warning, some ignore the warning and some reject the warning. Some people show an attitude of hatred towards a warning. Some disrespect the warning. Some of us just disobey the warning. If you disobey a traffic or road sign you might get penalized or hurt. It might even lead you to destruction. Warnings are very important to recognize. Some of us choose to do things our own way instead of consulting with God and obeying the warning signs. Some of us even think that it will be all right, even though it is not all right. We must abide by the rules and take heed to the warning signs. If you continue to do it your own way, it may be too late to get it right because you could be penalized or hurt to the point of death. Now I know you don't want to die now do you? Of course not! Let me tell you a story of how Israel refused to obey the Lord versus how we act and change when we really think we have found Mr. Right who is literally Mr. Wrong. So you decided to rebel, do your own thing and not believe God. Yes we do have some things in common with Israel.

> *Deuteronomy 1:32-36*
> *Yet in this thing ye did not believe*
> *the Lord your God, (verse 32)*
>
> *Who went in the way before you to*
> *search you out a place to pitch your*
> *tents in, in fire by night to shew you*
> *by what way ye should go, and in a*
> *cloud by day. (verse 33)*

*And the Lord heard the voice of your
words, and was wroth, and sware,
saying, (God hears you when you say
I can change him or her, NOT!)
(verse 34)*

*Surely there shall not one of these men
of this evil generation see that good
land, which I sware to give unto your
fathers, (verse 35)*

*Save Caleb the son of Jephunneh; he
shall see it, and to him will I give the
land that he hath trodden upon, and to
his children, because he hath wholly
followed the Lord. (verse 36)*

Oh baby doll, when you call yourself in love, there are
times when you will not listen to anybody. Even if you know
that they are trying to stop you from making a huge mistake
you still won't listen. This is exactly where the enemy wants
you. You will say things like, "Oh she's just jealous because
I got a man and she doesn't." My question is will it last after
all the warning signs you received? You may say, "She's just
upset because I get to eat at the finest restaurants." Baby, You
can probably count the times on one hand! Somebody else may
say, "She's just jealous because he chose me over her." I don't
think she wanted him anyway baby! You know some people
get real foolish and ignorant because of the lack of wisdom.
They may even say, "It is better to have a piece of a man than
not have any at all." Oh yeah? Well speak for yourself because

my preference is a whole man and not a piece of a man. Wait a minute, not only did you not believe your family or friends but you didn't even believe God.

God is the one who will go in and search the place out before you, to see if it's safe. He searches to see if it is safe for you to go into a relationship or not. He even searches your heart to see if you are ready. Now some things you don't have to ask God because you already know the answer to, like shacking up. You know that this is not Gods way, so then why are you doing it anyway? In some cases God will use fire to give you light. I am sure you don't want to deal with the fire sweethearts. I will advise you to acknowledge God before He even shows you the fire.

If you are the evil and wicked generation, then you will not see the good of the land. When we proceed to go into a relationship especially the wrong ones we tend to open our mouths and say some rough and tough things. We make comments like, "I don't care what they think, I am going to marry that man." "God is going to have to understand because my biological clock is ticking." I even heard one Pastor say, "My bible tells me that it is better to marry than to burn." Trust me sweethearts you have not felt burn until you enter into a wrong relationship. It can be any type of relationship such as a business, a church, a friendship or marriage. Suddenly you will see Mr. Right turning into Mr. All Wrong. Do you know why? The reason is because you chose with your flesh and you would not take heed to the warning signs.

Now God wants you to see the good of the land. Just because you are living with a man that is not your husband but yet he is paying your bills, this is not considered to be the good of the land. Listen, you will not see the good of the land as long as you are in an unholy relationship. That is why God said in verse 35, that there shall not one of these evil men of this generation that will see that good land. You can actually put a hold on your success or prosperity. But as long as you wholly and holy follow the Lord you shall see the good of the land.

When you begin to see the good of the land that means you are one of the best honey. That means that you are high quality, which means that you don't want to deal with any mess. You are suitable having the appropriate qualities to fit a particular purpose. You are skilled. You are gifted. You are virtuous having or showing an upright and virtuous character. You are honorable. You are valid. You are acceptable as true or genuine and sufficient for the purpose. You are helpful. You cannot be a help meet when someone knows it all and don't want to be helped. Ladies we do have that quality of being helpful. You are pleasant. You are beneficial to health or well being. You are favorable. You are obedient and well behaved. You are well mannered. You are somebody worth having.

No wonder you attract so many people. You attract the strange or wrong ones because they want what you got. Why wouldn't they want somebody that is worth having? You are somebody worth having. Do you hear me sweetheart? Say it, "I am somebody worth having." Say it again and again. You are precious baby. You are special! You belong to God! Don't allow anyone to put you or your children down. I don't know about you but I don't want to be in a relationship where somebody is just tolerating my children and me. Like L.L. Cool J. said, "I need love." If you don't love me then leave me alone and let me go! I do not want to be in a relationship with someone who does not love me! Farewell and goodbye!

Don't let them tell you that you are nobody. Don't let them tell you that you are not worth anything. You are Gods child! That makes you worth a whole lot!

So right now in the name of Jesus, I am calling you out! Those of you who are about to take that step towards matrimony, I am calling you out right now! You shall seek God in the mighty name of Jesus! Listen, I don't care how nice he or she is to you right now, seek God. I don't care how good the situation looks, you must seek God anyway for advice. I pray that you make the correct and right decisions for your life. If God say it is right then proceed. Go ahead and enter and have a good life in Jesus Name. Please be sure you are hearing from God, because some of us who say we heard from God actually did not hear from God at all. We heard from self. I've been there and done that.

One day I had just gotten off the computer and he was sleep. This was before the marriage. I got down on my knees and asked God about marrying this man. As I was about to end my prayer, I said, God if he is suppose to be my husband, then let him wake up and say, I love you very much and I'm going to marry you. I would pray to God like this from time to time for God to give me a sign. Right after I asked this of God, this man actually arose, awakened and said, "I love you very much and I am going to marry you." After he said that then he went right back to sleep. This startled me because I wasn't expecting it to happen that soon. All I could do is just look up at him in amazement because I was still kneeling at the time. Another reason why it startled me is because I said to myself there is no way he could have heard me because I wasn't praying out loud. In fact, I didn't open my mouth at all. I was praying silently on the inside. You know what I mean. So after that happened, I had my mind made up. My mind was made up that God said that he is to be my husband. I said to myself there is no way the devil could have done this because I was taught that the devil does not know what you are talking about unless you open your mouth. I was also taught that the enemy does not understand the spiritual language. I realize today that the enemy has a language also. For those of you who have made the wrong choices, you might as well look for a journey into the wilderness with many tears. Some of you have been longing for a trip anyway.

> *Deuteronomy 1:40-46*
> *But as for you, turn you and take your*
> *journey into the wilderness by way of*
> *the Red sea. (verse 40)*
>
> *Then ye answered and said unto me,*
> *We have sinned against the Lord, we*
> *will go up and fight, according to all*
> *that the Lord our God commanded us.*
> *And when ye had girded on every man*
> *his weapons of war, ye were ready to*
> *go up into the hill. (verse 41)*
>
> *And the Lord said unto me, Say unto*
> *them, Go not up, neither fight; for I*
> *am not among you; lest ye be smitten*
> *before your enemies. (verse 42)*
>
> *So I spake unto you; and ye would not*
> *hear, but rebelled against the*
> *commandment of the Lord, and went*
> *presumptuously up into the hill.*
> *(verse 43)*

*And the Amorites, which dwelt in
that mountain, came out against you,
and chased you, as bees do, and
destroyed you in Seir, even unto
Hormah. (verse 44)*

*And ye returned and wept before the
Lord; but the Lord would not hearken
to your voice, nor give ear unto you.
(verse 45)*

*So ye abode in Kadesh many days,
according unto the days that ye abode
there. (verse 46)*

If you choose to get in a wrong relationship, no matter how many warning signs you've received, then you automatically chose to turn and take the journey into the wilderness. Now that was your choice remember? Let me tell you, the wilderness is an uncomfortable situation. It is a place that makes you feel confused, overwhelmed, or desolate. You do know that Satan is the author of confusion right? If you didn't know now you know. If you are confused then Satan slipped in there somewhere. So with the bad choices you have made, you decided to become a sailor and begin the sea journey to depart or leave your harbor. You decided to leave your anchorage. I thought you were anchored in the Lord, what happened?

It looks like somebody avoided some warning signs. I know I did because I had all kinds of warning signs to stop. I looked over the signs and drove right through the stop sign. I'm sure many of you God showed you a stop sign and you didn't take heed to the warning sign. You kept going anyway. You didn't stop. You didn't stand still. You didn't take a chill pill. You didn't discontinue the relationship. You did not cease from moving, but yet you are supposed to be anchored in the Lord.

Some of us think that since we continued to go against Gods will anyway, we think we got what it takes to fight it or change them. Then we give all kinds of excuses why we think it is all right to go through the stop sign. I know what you are thinking. "I was in a hurry and I couldn't wait." "I'm running out of time because I am getting too old." Did you not know that sin separates? God tried to warn you but there was spiritual deafness. There were also rebellion and self-will blocking you from hearing from God. You have become powerless due to your disobedience. You will be defeated as long as you continue to live in sin. Some of you may say in your mind, "Well the invitations have been sent out so I might as well go through with it." "I don't want the people to think that we are crazy." You people pleaser! You ought to be trying to hear from God and please God and not people. The devil is a liar! Do you know that some of us even got the nerve to blame God and even cuss God for all the heartache and pain. You spoiled brat, God is not Burger King and you cannot have it your way unless you want to go through hell and high water. Now you can choose to have it your way anyway. If so, then don't blame God. It is your own fault for not taking heed to the warning signs! You need to make some better choices or you will reap the consequences. You need to wake up and stop sleeping with the enemy of misunderstanding. The enemy has got you confused. Wake up!

Some of you didn't just get tricked into marriage either. Some of you actually knew that your spouse was not equally yoked together with you but you did it anyway. That is not a joke! We think that we have so much power and anointing to fight that situation and change the man or woman to become what we want them to be. Your anointing is not enough to get you through a bad relationship. Now we may not confess that this is true, but in actuality this is deeply true. You do not have the power to change any man or woman. If you think you can, then you are headed for a big surprise, and that's what you get in cracker jacks. Surprise! The next thing you know is a surprise attack just hit you and hit you hard.

Now you have realized that you have made a bad decision after the honeymoon was over. So now you take your little proud self to Jesus and say, "Lord Jesus, I am very sorry that I have sinned, but I know that you are going to make everything all right." "I know you are going to use me to change him." "Amen." Then the Lord tells you, "No, no, no." "It's too late!" "You are living in all that sin and you wonder why your prayers are not answered?" "Don't you dare go home and fight, because I am not among you there." "You will mess around and get smitten." What does smite mean? I'm glad you asked that question. Smite means to hit hard. Honey, you might just get your feelings hurt and get knocked down at the same time. Smite also means to affect or afflict. It also means to become polluted. If you go home and try to fight for your rights, you will mess around and get hit hard. Being in a relationship like this will definitely affect you and afflict you.

Every time that I tried to fight for what was right, that demonic spirit would rise up against me because he didn't want to hear it. He would even threaten me. He would say, "You are lucky I love you because if I didn't, then I would have knocked you out." Now what kind of stuff is that? He would also brag about other women he actually hit. He thought it was funny. No one should ever threaten you like that! He thought they deserved it. That is sick! During the time that

I was writing this book, God gave me many dreams. Let me tell you about a dream that God gave me to actually let me experience the abuse that many other women are going through today.

Chapter 8
MY DREAM!

This dream let me truly feel the physical and mental abuse. It was also very emotional. This was truly an outer body experience. I was put in an abusive relationship in this dream and it seemed so real. There were three scenes and three different abusive situations.

Scene #1 consisted with me being at a gathering with a lot of people there sitting in rows and rows of chairs. Maybe it was a church function I am not sure, but while I was sitting there at the function or gathering my daughter was standing on my left side blocking my view of the door entrance. When I looked around her, I saw a man who I was afraid of so I tried to hide from him. I didn't tell anyone that I was afraid of him but I was. I told my daughter do not move because I didn't want him to find me or see me. She had no idea why I told her that. Well my daughter was so busy talking and mingling with the people that she really didn't hear me. She moved anyway and he spotted me right away. This man came charging at me and pulled at me as to say, "Come on, let's go!" To keep the confusion down, I departed with him. Not only was I fearful, but I was also embarrassed. For some reason I went with him anyway in silence knowing he was dangerous and unhealthy for me. I didn't want people to know so I kept it to myself.

Scene #2 involved me going to a club where the tables were set up and the people seemed to be laid back but yet drinking. When I got there, I spotted this particular man in the club that was very nicely dressed. That attracted me to him. You could tell that he was in a class all by himself, so I thought. He was sitting alone waiting on his next victim. He was wearing a very nice looking suit. Somehow I ended up sitting at his table with him. It was as if he was waiting for me to meet him there. It seemed like we had met before and had already started a relationship. Everything was moving so fast. We were talking and I was enjoying his company and conversation. This is a man I had been noticing for a while. I had my eye on him because I liked what I saw. I thought that he was a really nice man. In fact, I told some of my friends how nice I thought he was. He dressed nice, he smelled good and he had on nice shoes. (Little did I know that he really needed to change shoes! Change shoes! It is because he wasn't wearing the right shoes to keep the peace.) He seemed to have it going on with his outer appearance. I was thinking to myself, "Now he has class, he looks good and he has money." What did I know? I was thinking what a combination. In this dream I had my full senses. I could smell the alcohol and I could remember the dim lighting. As a matter of fact, it was kind of dark with an exception of the dance floor. He was a fine slim built man I was thinking. While I was thinking this, the next thing that happened came as a surprise and very sudden. This man began to attack me for no reason at all. He began to hit me. He began to pull on me and I could actually feel the hitting and pulling. He hit and pulled me so hard that it was so unbearable and unbelievable. I had my arms up trying to stop and block him from swinging on me. I told him over and over again that I told people that I thought you were so nice. I was thinking that this would make him stop. All he said was, "I am nice." He then pulled, yanked and dragged me out of the club without anyone ever saying a word or doing anything to stop him.

Scene #3 took place inside of a house. We were in the bedroom together, this man and I. Evidently I was in a relationship with this man because we had been sleeping together. That particular day, we had sex many times and now I was tired. I didn't want to have sex anymore. By this time he had already beat up on me but now he wanted to abuse me sexually. I said, "I don't want to have sex anymore." He asked me with a yell, "WHY NOT?" I said, "Because I am tired!" That didn't matter to him because he tried to force himself on me anyway. While he was still trying to force himself on me, another man that I knew came into the bedroom to help me. I guess he heard all the commotion. He was in the house all the time but in another room. When he entered the bedroom he spoke up and stood right in front of my abuser. My abuser was now standing at the end of the bed yelling at me and telling me that I am going to do what he said. The other man then said, "Man, she said she don't want to have anymore sex." My abuser then hit him and knocked him down. The other man then got back up and hit my abuser right dead in his face. It was a sucker punch and that was the end of him. He was out like a light.

Listen, somebody out there has experienced these situations and you know what I am talking about. You know that this is a dangerous and serious situation to be in. In fact, there may be someone going through this right now. If so, then Satan got you bound. Even if you fall you can get back up again. You can start over again. Maybe the enemy is holding you captive. Listen to me! This is not good! Do not keep this bottled up inside of you. You need to get help because no one should be putting his or her hands on you like that. Seek God on who you can confide in about your situation. It may not have escalated to the highest level yet but you shouldn't be in this type of situation. If you stay in an abusive relationship like this, then you may not come out alive. Help us Jesus!

Its time to wake up and really look at your situation clearly. Stay focused and speak these words, "I will not be stuck in bondage anymore no matter what the situation is and no matter what the circumstances are." "I can make it because I am the righteousness of God." I bind up fear in the name of Jesus. I loose love, power and a sound mind. Thank you Jesus for the victory! You will no longer be the victim but you will be the victor in Jesus name! I pray that you will come out of this dead relationship safely! Thank you Jesus! God will give you wisdom. My God is a just God. No matter how bad the situation or issue looks, you can come out on top with God.

In these dreams I had real feelings. I felt trapped. I felt like I was locked into a relationship and I couldn't get out. I had no idea what I was going to do. God allowed me to really feel the abuse. It is a terrible feeling and it hurts extremely bad. The pain was excruciating. I felt the hits and I had real fears. I was so disappointed and hurt that I allowed myself to get involved in such a relationship. When I had awakened from this dream, I literally cried out loud. When I cried out to God I said, "God, I have never felt or experienced something so real like that in my entire life. God then said to me, "*My people need to know that looks are deceiving.*" "*They need to know that appearances are deceiving.*" "*They need to know that it is not how nice the flesh is dressed up on the outside.*" "*This is how you get yourselves in trouble.*" He said, "*It happens all because you don't want to be alone and you are anxious.*" My God, please deliver anyone that is facing this type of dilemma right now! This is my prayer for the women all over the world right now! You must realize that there is more to a man than a nice suit. Lord, thank you for waking us up out of sleep!

I remember being in a relationship with a man that was so nice to me and very soft-spoken. I had never seen him get angry about anything. By no means was he a weak man but yet he seemed to be very humble. This was during the time when I was a partner with the devil. This was during the time I was clubbing it. I call myself doing the thing. We had the type of relationship where as we had an understanding. Let me show you a prime example of how we think we understand but don't have a clue. We made up our own rules. We were allowed to see whom we wanted to see but we will also see one another. Now when it came to us getting together, we would drop all the other relationships or dates until another day or time. Now he knew that if there was an unfamiliar car in my driveway, then don't knock on my door but keep going. This man really spoiled my children and I. My children really liked him, but what did they know? Well this went on for a while until one particular night he came by my house when I had company. I'm sure he saw the unfamiliar car in my driveway. Well he knocked on my door anyway. Now I couldn't figure out why this was happening. What was he thinking to be knocking on my door when we had an agreement? Well needless to say, he kept knocking on my door anyway but I never answered. He was determined to get in so he went on the side of my house. He went on the side where I had an air conditioner in the window. He knocked on my window and I stilled didn't answer. So the next thing that happened came as a surprise to me. Remember we talked about the enemy's surprise attacks. Honey you can hang out with the enemy all you want to but he doesn't like you. He is after you even though you are living worldly. It doesn't matter how he gets you, but he is coming after you whether you realize it or not. The devil comes to kill, still and destroy you. So be aware of whom you are hanging out with. Be aware of your surroundings. Don't partner up with the enemy. You need to get off the losing team and get on the winning team so you can have some protection. Then you can begin to make better choices in life.

Let's get back to the story. Since I didn't answer the knock on the door or the window, then guess what? He decided to take matters into his own hands. He actually pulled the air conditioner out of my window and climbed into my house. My company sat there and did nothing. After he climbed through the window, he then told me that he needed to talk to me. What could be that important that you have to pull my air conditioner out of my window? So I said what is it? You got me confused right now. We both went into the bathroom and he began to ask me why, why, why? I was saying why what? He then said, "Why did you do me like this?" Then he began to shake me and shake me until he finally hit me and ran out the house. The hit left a knot on the side of my head. I tried to cover it up with my hair but people noticed it anyway. He called me later to apologize. For a while I wouldn't take his calls. Every time he would call I would hang up. My brothers were upset about it. They would sit over my house waiting for him to come back over. One of my brothers said, "If he really loves you then he will be back and I will be sitting right here waiting for him." Finally I wanted to hear what he had to say. This is what he said, "I am very sorry but I fell in love with you and I got very jealous." He said, "I am very sorry but I didn't mean for this to happen." People, you need to know that this is not love! If a man puts his hands on you to harm you then he does not love you. Lets get this thing straight right now!

Apology is not enough and your actions are unacceptable. You have got to go! You must know that the enemy wants to confuse you about what love really is. Why? It is because he is the author of confusion. That is not love! The devil is a liar! At that time I was sleeping with the enemy of confusion and I didn't know it. Come on wake up, somebody! My God, please deliver anyone that is facing this type of dilemma right now! Lord, thank you for waking us up out of sleep! People this type of relationship could be life threatening.

In situations like this you could become so polluted with all their beliefs that you may even begin to compromise. What does it really mean to become polluted? It means that you and your family can become contaminated. Pollution can cause harm to an area of the natural environment. It can corrupt or defile you. It can make you morally or spiritually impure. If you are in the environment then don't let the environment get in you. So don't go home and try to fight for what you believe in. Just continue to pray and be the Christian that you are because if God is not going to help you fight there due to your disobedience, then your enemies can destroy you.

In the book of Deuteronomy 1:43 (found in chapter 7), even though God warned you not to go up in there like that, some of you still wouldn't listen. You are just hard headed! You just went up in there anyway like you are God, or like you heard from God. So since you went home with a nasty attitude, then the enemy who didn't want to hear a thing about God this, or God that, came out against you. He began to put you down and destroy you and it hurts. Then you began to cry out to God and He wouldn't answer you. He would not give ear to you because He had been trying to warn you all along. You wouldn't listen to Him. Now He won't answer you because you have been rebelling and being stubborn and just doing your own thing.

You just took yourself out of the will of God. You were living in sin and sin separates. So you had to deal with that issue for many days. I know it doesn't feel good at all. Been there done that! You suffered because you allowed it to happen in the first place. I must tell you that God will step in when He thinks you have had enough. That mountain has been in the way too long. Enough is enough!

> *Deuteronomy 2:1-3a*
> *Then we turned, and took our journey*
> *into the wilderness by the way of the*
> *Red sea, as the Lord spake unto me:*
> *and we compassed Mount Seir many*
> *days. (verse 1)*
>
> *And the Lord spake unto me, saying,*
> *(verse 2)*
>
> *Ye have compassed this mountain*
> *long enough: turn you northward.*
> *(verse 3a)*

Do you know what a compass is? It is a direction finder. It is personal direction and it is the scope of something such as a subject or area. You know how when you go to a place and scope things out. God will scope and observe the area of which and whom you were trying to attach yourself with. God knows that He has to give you personal direction. Why? It is because He has a purpose and plan for your life. He is the direction finder. God realizes that you have been going around the same mountain long enough. If you make a wrong turn somewhere, then God will and can lead you back in the right direction to ease the pain. This will allow you to get your peace back. You can get your happiness back. You can get your strength back. You can get your sense of direction back. You can get your strength back. No matter what dilemma you are in, just call on Jesus and He will see you through. Not in your own timing, but in Gods own timing. Thank you Jesus for stepping in when I needed you the most.

Chapter 9
MY PERSONAL WARNINGS

Now don't go and get all spooky on me. God comes to each and everyone of us in different ways. God can get a message to us in many ways. But the way my God revealed the warning signs to me, a little tiny baby could have understood. It was amazing but yet powerful and I will never forget it. I even asked myself over and over again, "How could you ignore signs like that?" Evidently I needed my license revoked since I couldn't obey the signs. Maybe you need to get a ticket and get your license suspended for awhile until you get things straightened out. You cannot violate the rules and think that disciplinary actions will not be taken. Well here's my story.

I was a hard working woman who met a hard working man. Not only was he a construction worker but he also worked at a graveyard. I had no idea that I was about to go through a graveyard experience. We developed a friendship. We began to do many things together. We went to several restaurants. We worked on business projects together in real estate. I was trying to move up the corporate ladder so he said that he would teach me whatever I needed to know about real estate. I wanted to find out more about purchasing homes so that I could rent them out or fix them up and possibly sell them if I choose to. Well needless to say, he was misleading. Now that should have been a sign in itself. He seemed to be a nice guy but he took me for a ride. I'm talking about a ride that led me into a lot of construction that nearly killed me.

Well, there were some other things we did together. We studied the bible. We began to pray together. We had even gone to church together. Hey, I really thought I had something. Here I met a man that attended church, prayed and studied his bible. Wow! I got it going on, right? Wrong! I thought I had it going on. I had even let this man destroy the radio ministry that God blessed me with. The devil had it out for me. Let me remind you that you don't have to be spiritual if you go to church. You don't have to be spiritual if you read your bible. You don't even have to be spiritual if you pray. Hard working does not make you spiritual even though that would be a plus in a holy relationship. Sometimes when we see that he is hard working, reads his bible, attends church and prays we tend to take our eyes off of spirituality. What it actually turned out to be was a prey. I know most of you agree that Satan is just another trick with a good rap (slang for conversation). And sometimes the rap ain't that good but you just get caught up in the moment.

Well one of my personal warning signs that God gave me was showing me a snake on the television quite a bit. Majority of the time it was when we were together. It would be one big snake on the screen. Sometimes it didn't even look like it fit with the program on TV. It happened enough times for me to notice it. Listen, a snake does not fit with your program at all. It doesn't matter who you are or who you think you are in God. We are still dealing with snakes from since the beginning of time when Eve was deceived. Many more will be deceived if we don't wake up and get some wisdom. A big snake, a little snake, or even a medium sized snake just does not fit. Why? I'll tell you why. It is because a snake means deception is coming your way. A snake is full of deception. They can deceive you into thinking that they really love the Lord with all their heart. Do you hear me? They can deceive you into thinking that they really love you when it is only a front. A snake is a threat to your life. A snake means danger, so get out of the way and let them pass you by. Stop, look and listen!

A snake has a lot of hatred. If you marry a snake, then he will hate you. I said he will hate you! It doesn't matter how nice you are to them a snake will hate you. You don't even have to do anything wrong. He will hate you anyway. A snake is simply a demon. A snake can cause you to be cursed with a curse. If you continue to stay under their covering, then they can cause you to be cursed with a curse. A snake means slander is coming. You will be talked about in your face and behind your back so get ready. A snake like person can cause damage to your reputation due to the lies that will be told about you. A snake is one having a critical spirit. A person with a critical spirit will find fault in everything that you do. They will constantly judge you. You know when there is a patient in the hospital and they tell you that they are in critical condition? That means that it is life threatening. Warning! A snake can be life threatening. A snake has evil intent. A snake intends to be evil because he has no intentions of being good. There is no good in a snake though they pretend to be good. A snake is a curse. A snake is literally cursed more than all cattle and more than every beast of the field. Be careful of any beast you may pick up or run into while working in the field.

> *And the Lord God said unto the serpent,*
> *Because thou hast done this, thou art*
> *cursed above all cattle, and above every*
> *beast of the field. Genesis 3:14a*

They have sharpened their tongues like
a serpent; adders, poison is under their
lips. (slander and evil speech)
Psalm 140:3

I have been in relationship after relationship where I was deceived. I was threatened. I was in danger and surely I was hated because there was no pure love. Slander and evil speech came against me. There were false and malicious things said against me. I literally experienced this. I could see the evil intent but I just kept on forgiving and giving him more chances to destroy me. After all, I had married the man by then. I wanted to be the Christian woman that I was known to be. I remember when I was a little girl. We used to say, "Sticks and stones may break my bones but words will never hurt." That statement is so untrue. I say that because some words can actually get you killed whether it is physical or spiritual.

Proverbs 23:32-33
At the last it bitteth like a serpent,
and stingeth like an adder,
(verse 32)

Thine eyes shall behold strange
women (someone who is not your
spouse), and thine heart shall utter
perverse things (lust). (verse 33)

Do not let anyone bite you like a serpent or sting you like an adder. What is an adder? My bible dictionary states that an adder is a venomous serpent. What is venomous? It is being full of malice, spite, or extreme hostility. Honey they will do things to you out of spite. Venomous is also being capable of inflicting a poisonous bite or sting. It is full of poison. Get the picture? Their eyes will also behold strange women, which means that they will lust after women who are not their spouse. Get this, their heart shall utter perverse things. Their lips may also utter perverse things. That means that it is already in their heart. It is a part of their character to willfully do wrong. So beware of snakes and remember that they do not fit into your program. It will do nothing but hinder you from your destiny. Stay away from snakes!

Another warning sign that I was given happened while sitting outside my mothers' driveway before I signed on the dotted line. We were conversing with one another. All of a sudden I saw a bunch of cats that came from nowhere. The cats almost filled the entire driveway. I have never in my life seen that many cats in one particular place. I have never known anybody that had cats at all in my neighborhood in all my years of living there. So you can't help but to notice something like that. Well let's find out something about cats.

What are the characteristics of a cat? I'm glad you asked that question. Cats are self-willed. They have a stubborn determination to hold to their personal views and behavior. Cats are very prideful and do whatever they want to do. I saw all of these symptoms in this marriage. Cats are not trainable. That means that they have an UN-teachable spirit. A person with this type of spirit has no desire to be taught righteousness. Why? It is because of their self-righteousness. Cats are predators and a predator is a ruthless aggressive person who is extremely determined or persistent. In other words, they will do whatever it takes to win you over. Listen, just because someone is persistent in choosing you, doesn't mean that you have to choose him or her. Please don't jump to conclusions before you find out what this person is filled with. You will find out what they are carrying if you choose to wait on God. My God, I pray that each person that read this book would wait on you Lord. I pray that they will begin to choose wisely. I pray that they will get and receive godly wisdom. I pray that if you fall after making a bad choice, then get back up again. These things I pray in Jesus Name. Thank you for the victory Lord!

Let me open up your understanding to more of the cat's characteristics. There are other characteristics of a cat as if that wasn't enough. They have an unclean spirit. If a person has an unclean spirit, then that means that they are nasty and dirty. They will treat you dirty because they are dirty. They are sinful. So if they are dirty and sinful then they are quick to commit a sexual sin. They are religiously impure. Let me say that again. They are religiously impure. Honey, they could care less about spiritual or religious rules, yet they have this charm down packed. I mean packed on ice because they are ice cold. They are very crafty with this charm that they not only can fool you, but they can fool your family, friends, church members and Pastors. Cats have a bewitching charm (witchcraft). Yes cats are sneaky and crafty. Cats are deceptive. They can also present self-pity to you very well. They can even fake a cry. I tell you they got it down packed. I'm sure you have seen some of the two-legged cats walking the streets spitting (speaking) nothing but game. They call them the cat daddies.

> *Proverbs 7:10-12, 21*
> *And, behold, there met him a woman*
> *with the attire of an harlot, and subtil*
> *of heart. (verse 10)*
>
> *(She is loud and stubborn, her feet*
> *abide not in her house; (verse 11)*

Now is she without, now in the streets,
and lieth in wait at every corner.)
(verse 12)

With her much fair speech she caused
him to yield, with the flattering of her
lips (purring like a cat) she forced him.
(verse 21)

Beware of the cool cat daddies that you decide to embrace. They just might be hazardous to your health. I'm speaking of the cat daddies who love to roam the streets. They talk the talk and they walk the walk always headed to mischief. They never want to stay at home. They never want to show accountability because they are up to no good. Now let me flip the script because there are women that are just as bad. I don't want the women to feel left out. I'm speaking of the women who are never satisfied because of the lust spirit that has attached itself to them. Honey, they roam the streets looking for their next victim. I know because back in the day, I did the same thing. Now remember, if a cat is not trainable and has an UN-teachable spirit, they are not trying to hear you or the Pastor. They are too busy trying to do their own thing but yet keep you saved. The cat is full of craftiness so it may take the very elect a moment to figure them out. You will get played like a "funky piano." They will show you self-pity while acting like they are all for you but in reality they are not at all for you. They are for themselves only. Their focus is what they can gain from you because they are predators.

My next warning was very strange to me. Now I told you not to get spooky on me. Check it out. As a child, I have always had some strange spiritual gifts that I decided not to tell people because some people just don't understand. Some people are just not ready for it because they lack understanding. But since God inspired me to write this book and put my business out there, then I must be obedient to God. God said that people could read my personal experiences and make a strong decision not to go through what I have gone through.

Now this warning began with me and my soon to be spouse sitting in his van in my mothers driveway again. We were talking and began to open up to one another concerning our background. In the midst of listening to him, I saw something. I was looking at him while he was talking and his face literally changed into three different things. His face changed before my very eyes. It changed into (1) a bull, (2) a pig, and (3) a drunk or drug addict. At that time I didn't have enough sense to keep it to myself. I just didn't know any better. I didn't realize that this information was for me and not him. I should have excused myself to the bathroom only never to come back. So I decided to tell him what I saw. Me and my, big mouth! The face changes were so clear to me. I began to ask him, "Were you ever a drunk?" "Are you stubborn?"

You need to know what each one of these faces represent and what I dealt with in the home. For the most part, if you look into somebody's face the face actually shows what is in his or her heart. If you are sad your face shows it. If you are glad your face shows it. If you are mad your face shows it. If you are bad your face shows it. If you don't like the way something tastes your face shows it. If you are dealing with someone that never shows any expression then beware because they could be wearing a mask. Now the mask is one of the enemy's secret weapons because he loves to disguise himself. Some people wear a mask over the face to prevent recognition. A mask can hide someone's true motives or feelings. In this marriage I dealt with a lot of hidden motives.

THE BULL:

Let's begin with the bull. The bull actually means persecution is on the way. It means get ready for spiritual warfare. It means get ready for opposition. It means get ready for slander. Wow! Another dose of slander, huh? It means get ready for accusation. Honey, it was a constant battle. A bullheaded person is a threat to you. In other words, a bull is a sign of danger that something undesirable is going to happen. It means that this particular person is likely to cause you harm and pain. I never desired to go through any pain like that. I never want to go through anything like that ever again. I was accused of so many things. There was always opposition concerning the beliefs of God. I was persecuted daily. I was afflicted and tormented because of his seem to be hatred of Christ and godly living.

> *Psalms 22:12-13*
> *Many bulls have compassed: (scoped,*
> *looked at or examined) me: strong*
> *bulls of Bashan have beset me round.*
> *(verse 12)*
>
> *They gaped (to open wide) upon me*
> *with their mouths, as ravening (to eat*
> *something voraciously or greedily)*
> *and roaring lion. (verse 13)*

This type of spirit causes confusion and disorder. When you see red flags like this, then it is a sign of how somebody or something will fare in the future. The strong bulls will try to devour you like a roaring lion. A lion is nothing but a big wild predatory cat. Oh yes, he is a large wild member of the cat family. These cats are brave, strong and fierce. They don't scare easily at all. Oh yes, they will open their mouths wide to eat you alive because they are violent. They could care less about the PoPo's. (slang for Police) The bull is the soul enemy. They will try to dig a pit for your soul. They will take your treasure and precious things. Satan desires to have you. He wants to sift you as wheat. He is walking around seeking whom he can devour. He will try his best to stop you from seeking God because that is his intentions. He wants to stop you from loving God. He wants to stop you from serving and worshiping God. He does not want you to keep God's laws. He will try his best to stop you from obeying God and getting wisdom. He is determined to keep you in a certain environment so that the environment can get in you. What kind of environment is that? It is an evil environment with fleshly lust, sin, adultery, ignorance, evil men and hell! God was trying to let me know by showing me the signs to warn me for what to expect in the near future. I was one that noticed the signs but ignored them. I drove straight through the stop sign.

THE PIG:

Now lets approach the second facial expression that I saw which was the pig or swine. A pig is unclean. A pig is selfish. Listen, there were many times that we went to a restaurant and I could never sit where I wanted to sit because of his selfishness. It was all about him choosing his seat even if I had taken a seat already. He literally wanted me to get up so that he could sit on a particular side. He could care less about how I felt and where I wanted to sit. That was ridiculous! A pig or swine could be a backslider or an unbeliever. Why do I say that? It is because after the honeymoon was over, he really didn't want God in the house. It was all a front. It was as if he was saying, lets keep God in the church only on Sunday morning. I was not used to that. So now I'm thinking, "If he was a believer then when did he backslide?" "Was it during the honeymoon or was it there all the time?" "Was he ever a believer?" I had to learn that the spirit that was influencing him was never satisfied and it is all because pigs are greedy. They constantly eat junk food. A pig or swine is also a fornicator and an adulterer. Listen, if he is never satisfied, then of course he will fornicate or commit adultery easily. Listen, he was drawn away by his own lust and got pregnant with it. So when lust was conceived it brought forth sin and sin when it is finished it brings forth death. Believe me, I was in a dead relationship.

Listen, a swine is an idolater. That means that one worships idols. A person could worship their job and money over God. If they do then that job or money becomes their god. A person is enticed by idols due to their corrupt heart. Now this causes separation already because 1 Corinthians 5:11 reads, "But now I have written unto you not to keep company, if any man that is called a brother (a spiritual companion or a fellow Christian) be a fornicator, or covetous, or and idolater, or a railer (a rebellious person), or a drunkard, or and extortioner (one who obtains by threats); with such an one no not to eat." We are not to let this junk food be served on our plate. Sometimes it happens because of their false profession and unjust gain. You may even begin to idolize this man without even realizing it. Christians are warned against keeping company with this type of person. The bible tells us to flee from. The bible also tells us that there should be no fellowship with, keep from and turn from. So now if I choose to marry this person anyway then my marriage is already over even before I enter and sign the contract. That means that we will enter into the marriage already separated and divided. Amos 3: 3 reads, "Can two walk together, except they be agreed?" Are you both walking with God? I cannot pray against the will of God. I just can't do that! I chose to drive through the stop sign and not take heed. That is why I experienced so much mess.

A pig is also a hypocrite. A hypocrite pretends to be what one is not. A hypocrite also pretends to believe what one does not believe. That's why I pray that you slow down because we have a lot of pretenders out here. The enemy is not playing. It is time to pull the covers off this fool! The devil is a liar and the father of it! I bind the enemy and his lies up right now and loose the spirit of truth, in Jesus Name.

The pig is also a persecutor. A persecutor is one that harasses you continually. You will be afflicted, oppressed and tormented because of their sinful nature. This will happen because of the hatred for God. This will happen because of the ignorance of God. My bible tells me that we must pray through persecution but as long as it continues then God said you are going to have to flee. Now you can stay in this type of relationship if you want to but I am going to be obedient to God when he tells me to flee. The swine is also vicious, meaning they intend to do harm like a vicious dog. They will display immoral behavior. They will show fierce violence. They are dangerous and aggressive. They are unsound meaning incorrect or showing faulty logic. He or she is vengeful and hostile to virtue. A swine represents danger. Listen, ask God for spiritual vision and discernment because we ought to be able to recognize a gross man or woman. I pray that you recognize someone who despises you.

Give not that which is holy unto the dogs, neither cast ye your pearls before swine, lest they trample them under their feet, and turn again and rend you. Matthew 7:6

Do not compromise and give your holiness to the dogs. You are a precious gem. You are a pearl. You are somebody that is considered to be valuable and beautiful. You are precious and unique in your own way. You ought to be treated with care. They ought to use affection when talking with you because you are somebody. Don't let the dogs dog you out! Who let the dogs out anyway? Somebody please tell me where is the dogcatcher? We have some stray dogs on the loose. Beware of wolves in sheep clothing. A wolf is greedy and cruel and a wolf will eat you alive. A wolf will hunt you down and pursue you with aggression as if they are so much in love with you. They may look harmless or pleasant but is in fact dangerous or unpleasant. A dog is a domestic animal and domestic violence is in them whether they let it be known or not. So don't get surprised when the violence starts. Don't let anybody hit you because this is not a sign of love! Do not let the pigs walk all over you. Don't let them destroy or injure you. If they see that you will allow them to walk all over you then they may turn around and attack you forcefully, mentally, physically, emotionally or spiritually. Don't let them cause you pain or distress to your heart or emotions. If you keep letting them walk all over you they will rip you apart eventually.

2 Timothy 3:1-7
This know also, that in the last days perilous (physical or spiritual danger) times shall come. (verse 1)

MY PERSONAL WARNINGS

*For men shall be lovers of their own
selves, covetous, boasters, proud,
blasphemers, disobedient to parents,
unthankful, unholy, (verse 2)*

*without natural affection, trucebreakers
(violators of an agreement), false
accusers, incontinent (uncontrolled
indulgence of the passions), fierce,
despisers of those that are good (hostile
to virtue). (verse 3)*

*Traitors (one who betrays a trust), heady
(conceited), high minded (self righteous
spirit), lovers of pleasures more than
lovers of God; (verse 4)*

*Having a form of godliness, but denying
the power thereof: from such turn away.
(verse 5)*

*For of this sort are they which creep into
houses, and lead captive silly women
laden with sins, led away with divers
lusts, (verse 6)*

*Ever learning, and never able to come
to the knowledge of the truth (dull in
hearing and have spiritual ignorance).
(verse 7)*

Now if you are not taking heed to Gods warnings you
could be in big trouble. If your spouse is dull of hearing and

have spiritual ignorance, where do you think you will be headed? I'll tell you. You will be headed for a ditch! If you let the blind lead you, then you will be headed for destruction! There are a lot of people that have a form of godliness, but deny the power thereof. They are forever learning and never able to come to the knowledge of the truth. They are just dull in hearing and having spiritual ignorance. We are living in perilous times where men are lovers of their own selves. They brag and boast about what they do. They are so prideful and disobedient. They are disobedient to their parents, your parents and anybody else parents. Do not let the Pharisees lead you! Do you know any Pharisees? Are you in a relationship with a Pharisee? Who are the Pharisees anyway? I'm glad you asked that question. The Pharisees are upholders of tradition. Are any of you upholders of tradition? Maybe you are a Pharisee yourself. Maybe you teach your sons to be a player out of tradition and you are proud of it. Maybe you teach your daughter to disrespect her elders out of tradition. Honey, some of these parents today will allow their children to cuss another parent out. That is unheard of. That is crazy! No respect at all and this is how they are raised. Maybe your parents taught you to lie and you are upholding that tradition. What traditions are you upholding that could lead you to a ditch? You better let those Pharisees alone.

> *Let them (Pharisees) alone: they be*
> *the blind leaders (the head) of the*
> *blind. And if the blind lead the blind,*
> *both shall fall into the ditch.*
> *Matthew 15:14*

Blindness is destitute of sight, physical or spiritual. What causes blindness? Disobedience causes blindness and disobedience is hooked up with the enemy. If you got the blind leading you or if you must submit to someone whom is blind, then your vision will become destitute. If this happens, then you will lack necessities of life. Try not to choose someone who is blind because this can cause you to become blind and fall into a ditch with them.

THE DRUG ADDICT:

The third and last facial expression I saw was a drunk or drug addict. Now a drunk or someone that is doing drugs equals influenced. Now you can be drunk in two ways. (1) Under the influence of the Holy Spirit, which is wise, or (2) under the influence of drugs or alcohol, which is of a demonic spirit, which is foolish. You need to choose wisdom over foolishness. If you continue to indulge with drunkenness of alcohol and/or drugs, then you will be influenced by the enemy. This is not good. A lot of times you will not have control of what you do because you have allowed the enemy to lock you into witchcraft. The enemy makes it feel real good to you when you are under the influence. You need to know that you tend to make poor decisions when the enemy is controlling you. The enemy can influence you to do many things while under the influence of drugs and alcohol.

There are so many people that are under the influence of a Jezebel spirit. This type of person operates in a controlling and manipulative way. Let me inform you that a person that operates out of the Jezebel spirit can be a man or a woman. The Strong Concordance states that Jezebel means UN-husbanded. Even though they were married, their lack of submission and their infidelities proved that true marriage meant nothing to them. They worship idols and persecute the prophets of God. This type of spirit seeks to lead you to a dead end so that you will never fulfill the call of God on your life. Once a person with the Jezebel spirit express loyalty to you, they will soon do an about face. They dislike any demands for accuracy or accountability. Rarely will they admit an error. There were times that I would say to my spouse after a terrible argument, "Honey, I'm sorry." "I admit that I was wrong so I do apologize." Do you think that he would ever admit that he was wrong? I don't think so! Individuals with a Jezebel spirit are skilled in getting their way. They will find all kinds of ways to manipulate or control you. This spirit can destroy families.

The enemy can influence you to do many things while under the influence of drugs and alcohol addiction. Things you would not ordinarily do whether you are a Christian or not. You know what I mean. There are just some things you know you wouldn't ordinarily do! Yet while you are in this state of mind, it is as if you are under a spell that you cannot snap out of it. It's like being stuck on stupid. Instead of singing the song, "I am stuck on Band-Aid cause Band-Aid stuck on me," you will be singing another song. You may need to cover some scars and some wounds if you are locked into a relationship like this. If you stay in an abusive relationship when God clearly states for you to GET OUT, then your song becomes "I am stuck on Stupid cause Stupid stuck on me!" Go ahead and laugh about it, but I was there. I was there! The enemy enjoys having you under his control. When the enemy has you under his control, you will become a fool for him. He will then teach you to become selfish, rebellious, more self-indulging, proud, conceited, arrogant, boastful and unchangeable if you have not already picked up these attributes. These are attributes of the enemy. Now all these things will feel so good to your flesh that it will cause an addiction.

*A wise man feareth, and departeth
from evil: but the fool (drunk or
drug addict) rageth, and is confident
(arrogant and boastful).
Proverbs 14:16*

*The way of a fool (drunk or drug
addict) is right in his own eyes:
(conceited and self righteous) but
he that hearkeneth unto counsel is
wise. Proverbs 12:15*

I don't care how much a person tries to cover their foolishness, it will show eventually. The slip up will come. If you can't seem to make wise choices on your own, then get you some wise counsel. Try to choose someone who will not put all your business out in the streets. Now I was no perfect angel and I began to compromise the word of God. I knew better but I did it anyway. My excuse for compromising was because of the many lies my spouse told me. I never knew when he was lying to me or telling me the truth. His word meant nothing. I mean nothing! I also felt alone even though I was married. He would leave me many times home alone. I could be sleep and wake up and he would be gone. I could be in the kitchen and walk through the house only to find out that he was gone. I could be in the back yard with him and he would walk through the house, as if he was going to get something to drink but instead go right out the front door and leave. I would call him on his cell phone and he would sometimes hang up on me or yell at me. I became very confused on what to do since prayer didn't seem to help at the time. Even though I was clinging to the book, "The Power of a Praying Wife," there was still no power. The enemy was working me over time. I was tempted to do all sorts of evil to get back at him.

Overcoming Temptation

What is temptation? It is an enticement to do wrong. I was very enticed to do wrong to him for treating me the way that he did. My focus was so strong on what should I do about him or what should I do to him. Now there is a flip side of enticement that will cause you to enter into temptation of a bad relationship. Enticement is something very desirable and hard to resist. We have entices that allure you to evil. Now when you are being allured that means that they use charm or an attraction. Have you ever met anybody or anything that is charming? Charming people are fascinating aren't they? A new house, a new pair of shoes, a new dress, etc. are fascinating aren't they? Do they make you smile? Well of course they do. Does it make you want to have it badly? Well of course it does. Do they give you money? Well of course they do. That's just to set the trap.

A lot of times charm always seem to attract people. Ladies lets keep it real now. When you see a fine charming man you can't help but to look at him. It's as if you are spellbound. It's as if they have cast a spell on you. Be careful because this so-called charm that is alluring you in can actually throw you off course. Then you won't really be able to see spiritually what's inside that person. They could be wicked and deceiving. So be very careful people. Are you careful? Please be very careful and cautious.

Allure is a highly attractive quality. It is an attractive or tempting quality possessed by somebody or something. It could be a city, money, control, pornography, television, a man or women. Listen, a man doesn't even have to be good looking to posses an attractive quality. Maybe you like the fact that he has a lot of money and he's willing to give you some of it. Let's keep it real ladies. What is it that has your attention and is taking you off course with God? It has to be something that is attractive to you. Now some of these things may tempt or entice you to do the wrong things. If so, then it is because you are attractive to it or because you are trying to keep up with the Jones'. Maybe it has become your idol and your god. Since it is so desirable then it becomes hard to resist. That's what charm can do for you. We must stop the charm spell.

Chapter 10
LIVING OVERSEAS

While living overseas with my husband and children, I was fed up with the fact that my husband turned his back on God. I continued to pray, read my bible, and make sure that he had lunch ready every time he came home for lunch. Before he would return for work after lunch, I would gather the children and we would all stand in a circle to pray for his protection, since he was in the military. I wasn't working at the time. After a while I could tell that he was not so interested in praying anymore like he used to be. After a period of time this discouraged me. I began to get weak. I would walk through the house preaching to a crowd of people that wasn't there. I would study my bible and preach to the furniture and the walls. I would do this through the house while he was away. Each day I was getting weaker and weaker while watching his negative attitude. The enemy was working me overtime. Things were occurring that caused me to lose trust in my husband.

One day I said, "I am tired of sleeping and laying around the house doing the same thing over and over again." I said, "I am going to work." He actually didn't want me to work at first. Finally I did it anyway. While working in Nuremberg Germany, my husband and I purchased a charcoal gray BMW together. Since I didn't have my German license yet, the car had to be put in his name only. Now I didn't have a problem with that because I trusted him enough to know that even though the car was in his name, the car still belonged to the both of us. So one day my husband said to me with a loud voice, "This is not your car anyway, because my name is the only name on this car!" I looked at him and I thought to myself, "Okay, you want to play games?" "Then let the games begin."

That hurt me and I was wondering how could he say such a thing. It hurt me because I never expected him to approach me like that. I then learned how to drive a manual. I also got my German license. Then I began to drive myself to work with a rental car. While working, I was still in pain from all the things that was going on in my relationship at home. I began to feel sorry for myself. I was just a big baby. Then the enemy began to put thoughts in my mind. Oh yes, the enemy played mind games with me. The enemy brought up the fact that in the past you forgave him for cheating on you with someone who was supposed to be your friend. I never once cast down the imagination. I just let it grow. I kept thinking, he betrayed my trust. Oh how that hurt! To me, he just continued to take me for granted.

Listen, I knew that I shouldn't have looked back. I knew that looking back and dwelling on the past could destroy me. I looked back anyway. I just started thinking about everything he did to me that I didn't like. At this time, the enemy had put me in sleep mode. I had become unconscious of the things that was truly surrounding me. Soon after that, I met a Sergeant that I could "relate to." I needed to talk to somebody. My husband and I were not communicating so well at the time. Does this sound familiar? Now honestly, I loved my husband with all my heart, not part but all of my heart. At this particular time in my life, I was given up on him. All the years we had been together, I had never once cheated on him and yet he took me for granted. Those were my thoughts constantly.

Hmmm, I have to laugh a little because here I am trying to justify what I was now going to do next. It still doesn't make it right. So since I was hurting, I had decided to use the other man to help soothe my pain. I met this Sergeant that had charm and style. He became the dark chocolate good-looking man that gave me the attention that I wanted and needed. The shade of his skin was the complete opposite from my husbands. Really he wasn't my type but I compromised my type for the attention that I wanted. To tell you the truth, I didn't have a clue on what my type should be. I was just out for revenge. The enemy had me in sleep mode. This is not a good thing. Do not compromise! This man spoke with me about his relationship and I spoke to him about mine. I told him that it hurt me that my husband did me the way that he did concerning the car we purchased. This was so foolish of me to open up like that to someone I didn't really know. This not only placed me in sleep mode, but it also placed me in victim mode. I have allowed myself to become a victim of circumstances. The issue about the car seems petty doesn't it? The enemy made it look like such a big thing to me. I was seriously hurt. My new friend seemed to understand my hurt. We seemed to communicate very well. He also seemed to listen very well.

His charm attracted me. So one day to my surprise, he came up to me and told me that he had a friend that was going TDY or leaving. Then he said that his friend had a "BMW" that he was going to leave him to sell. My eyes got big and said, "Really?" I then asked him, "How much is it going to cost?" He said, "I don't know, but you can get it." I was really excited about this. Days past, then one day the Sergeant approached me to tell me that he was going to park the car across the street from the PX. I said, "Okay." He then proceeded to tell me that he would leave the keys inside the car. He also said that he wanted me to listen to the cassette tape that he had made for me. Finally he said, "I want you to tell your husband that you paid five hundred dollars for it." I agreed.

Can you see how temptation can overtake you so easily if you don't watch it or conquer it? Now it should have never escalated to this level, because remember, I was still married. That was completely out of order. The enemy will always find some way to tempt you. At that time I said this is just what the doctor ordered. Well doctor Jesus didn't order this for me because he wants me to live and not die. Here I am allowing the enemy to not only take my marriage, but also take my life.

I was getting deeper and deeper in sleep mode. I was on my way to being totally unconscious. I was probably snoring by then. I had got to the point of being lazy and ignorant about it. You may say, I needed to do something to pay him back before I go crazy, but it is not about paying anybody back. It is not my place to do so. Vengeance is mine, said the Lord. Let God handle your situation in the home before you get wrapped up, tied up or tangled up in something you may be sorry for later.

We got up one Saturday morning and I told my husband, "Lets go to the PX." He was willing. When we got there, I told him, "Pull across the street near the orange BMW with the sunroof." He did as I asked. I then immediately got out, ran to the car, opened the door, got the keys, adjusted the seat and started the car. He said, "What are you doing?" I then said, "This is my car!" I said it loud like he did before. Now I'm not going to lie, it really felt good to say that. Doesn't it seem like these great offers couldn't have come at a better time? Because of my situation, it seemed to be on time. You must remember that there is a flip side to that. This is how the enemy allures you or entices you to come on into his territory.

Yet I was still saying to myself, this man barely even know me, but yet he gave me a car? He didn't just give me a car, but he gave me a BMW with a sunroof and a ready-made cassette tape with love songs on it. Was this really free? Believe me he had other ideas in mind. That's why we must overcome temptation. So how do we overcome temptation? First we need to know what it means to overcome something. Overcome means to conquer. Now we all have struggles with temptation and we all have difficulty with temptation sometimes but how can we overcome or conquer it? Some of us really need to runaway fast from temptation and never look back. It doesn't matter how good it looks to you but make sure you got your running shoes on in order to keep the peace.

> *I Corinthians 9:26-27*
> *I therefore so run, not as uncertainly*
> *So I fight not as one that beateth the*
> *air (verse 26)*

In other words, in this Christian race, You shouldn't run without a goal and you shouldn't fight or box your fists in the air when there is spiritual warfare. This is not the way we fight in spiritual warfare because we are fighting the enemy. We are talking about invisible foes. We must prepare to fight with Gods armor on at all times. We need Gods word. We need to keep the faith. We need to know Gods promises and stand on them. Avoid worldly entanglements and preys. Remember to pray continuously.

You must also deny yourself (refuse yourself, refuse to acknowledge yourself, do not allow yourself the gratification by serving your selfish needs or desires). Even if it is offered, decline to accept it. Tell yourself NO! I didn't deny myself and I didn't tell myself no. I did not control my own behavior because I was serving my own selfish needs and desires. You must also endure hardness (survive it even when it gets hard). You must be self-controlled (you must have the ability to control your own behavior, especially in terms of reactions and impulses). You should be alert (be watchful and ready to deal with whatever happens). Make sure that you wear your whole armor.

> *But I keep under my body, and bring*
> *it into subjection: lest that by any*
> *means, when I have preached to others*
> *I myself should be a castaway.*
> *1 Corinthians 9: 27*

We need self-control. We need to restrain some of our appetites. Some of us crave too much junk food. We must come out of self-denial. Saying that I don't have any problems with my flesh simply puts me into self-denial because that is a lie. We all have struggles with our flesh from day to day. Why do the bible say mortify the flesh? This is a daily process. We must kill the flesh daily or else you could become a castaway. Trust me, your flesh will rise to things that it want and shouldn't have, so you have to kill it. I must keep my body under control. You must keep your body under control so that you will not lose out or become a castaway. A castaway is a person that's worthless. God cannot really use you because people will look at you and see a person that is shipwrecked. If you do not put your body up under subjection, you will begin to sink. Don't you know that you could become very damaging to yourself and to others by failing to control yourself?

Without a doubt temptation is going to come to you and me. Just because you go to church every Sunday and you read your bible all the time, does not mean that temptation has ended for you. Just because you preach the word does not mean that temptation has ended for you. Temptation has not ended because you may be anointed and you know the scriptures by heart. Temptation has not ended because you are friends with the Pastor. After all that, temptation is going to come and you must bring your body up under subjection because your flesh will not do it. Your flesh will say yum yum eat em up! Some of us think we are so heavy spiritually that we don't have to consider this, but you are absolutely wrong!

Luke 7:32 reads, "Remember Lots wife." I know you know the story of the day God decided to destroy the city of Sodom and Gomorrah because of all the wickedness. He told Abraham's nephew Lot, to take his wife and children and run and don't look back. Lots wife was disobedient and looked back anyway which destroyed her. She turned into a pillar of salt. Now I know you don't want to sacrifice your life by tasting destruction, so remember Lots wife. She looked back and was destroyed. That is the problem with some of us today, we keep looking back saying, I remember when my husband cheated on me. Some of you are still bitter and are holding grudges. Then you enter into another marriage blaming your new husband for what your last husband did to you. Remember Lots wife. I remember what Pastor Oops did to me. Then you start blaming every Pastor for being that way. Remember Lots wife. I remember what happened to me when I was a little girl. Remember Lots wife. I remember when I used to be a player. Well maybe you used to be a young player with lots and lots of women. Then God delivered you from that. Now you are thinking of becoming an old player with lots and lots of women. Remember Lots wife. I remember when my son was on crack and he stole everything from me. Remember Lots wife and don't look back because this could destroy you if you continue to dwell on it.

Now how can we keep our bodies up under subjection? I'm glad you asked that question. One way is to discipline yourself. If while at home you get the remote and turn it to the music videos and it causes you to become lustful, then don't watch it anymore. You need to be conscious and have control over your lifestyle. Another way is to fast and pray. Everybody likes to eat but nobody likes to fast and pray. Sometimes you may not even feel like praying but you should discipline yourself to do so anyway.

Chapter 11
OUT OF CONTROL

Speaking of control and discipline, somehow this drug they call crack has gotten out of control. Now just because I am addressing this drug does not mean I am putting anyone down or condemning anyone because most of us have been addicted to something and it doesn't have to be drugs or alcohol. What makes any of us better than them when we were addicted to a man. Now ladies when some of you are addicted to a man, you tend to act out of character. I am addressing this particular drug because someone very dear to me has been fighting or struggling with this addiction. I'm sure some of it had to do with a lack of discipline because they didn't deny themselves. They didn't bring their bodies up under subjection.

I'm sure some people have looked at the drug user as being shipwrecked. I'm sure some people probably wanted to cast them away, but they had no control, so don't give up on them. Remember that God can change anyone, but you cannot change anyone! Now it will definitely help if you fast and pray for them. I have realized that somehow this drug they call crack has a certain attraction that is deceiving a lot of our people today. Do you know anybody that has been deceived by this drug? Yes I have, and trust me, it is very painful when it is someone very close to you. I believe that it had to begin with a charmer. Evidently it brought about an attraction for the drug dealer to make some quick money.

Now ladies what about a man dealing himself to you in order to make some quick money or maybe he or you just might want to take a quick hit of sexual satisfaction. Sex can become your drug. A man can become your drug. A woman can become your drug. Your vehicle can become your drug. Your house can become your drug. Your job can become your drug. Watching television can become your drug. Lying can become your drug. Stealing can become your drug. Gossiping can become your drug. And the list goes on and on. These drugs also brought about an attraction to the drug user by the power of persuasion. Neither one are winners. They all are losers until they are delivered from this deadly crime.

This drug like any other drug can cause physical as well as a spiritual death. Maybe the attractive feature delights the both of them. With the drug dealer, maybe it makes them feel powerful and in control even though the enemy is controlling them while they are clocking dollars or giving you a hit of satisfaction. They don't realize that the enemy has put them in sleep mode. And in most cases they don't realize that this is a dangerous state to be in. It is best to get out now before it is too late because you will be held responsible for every life you have destroyed. What about the male drug dealer that is trying to sell you sexual sins or lust ladies? What about the female drug dealer that is trying to sell you sexual sins or lust men? This has happened in many cases while there is a spouse and children at home. You will be held responsible for every bad decision that you make. Wake up! You have been oversleeping! Don't be late for your appointment!

With the drug user, maybe it makes them feel good and possibly help them to forget about their troubles. You may or may not know that the enemy has placed you in sleep mode during this time. I have experienced someone who was close to me that got sucked up into this drug called crack as if they were up under a spell. I have never heard any preachers or

Pastors teach or address this issue in depth in the church. So I decided to do the research for myself since I had to deal with this issue myself.

I asked the question, "What is crack?" I know it exists, but yet I don't know much about it. I have never heard anybody preach in detail about it in church, but yet it is destroying our families. I am very concerned about that! Now most of us know somebody who is or was on crack. I'm sure some of them are very dear to you. It could be a mother or father. It could be a brother or sister. It could a cousin or friend. It could even be a husband or wife.

So what is it and why is it so popular? Lets look at the dictionary definition.

1) Crack is a purified and extremely addictive form of cocaine,
2) Crack means to break or make something break,
3) Crack means to break into pieces,
4) Crack means to hit hard, to hit something with a powerful impact,
5) Crack means to fail or make something fail. It means to fall, give way or breakdown, or to make somebody or something do so,
6) Crack means to breakdown psychologically, or to cause somebody to break down, psychologically,
7) Crack means to force a way into something, especially a safe or safe place of yours.

Crack is one of the most popular drugs around that are destroying our families. Our families are breaking because of this drug or destroyer. Maybe once upon a time you trusted this individual that was doing drugs and you felt safe. Since they became addicted to this drug you no longer felt safe anymore. If you have dealt with this issue before then you know that you never know what to expect next from them. It causes family hearts to be broken into pieces. I'm sure it hurts you to see your family or friend in this state. This destroyer or drug hits you hard and has a powerful impact on you when someone that is dear to you is using this drug. If you or someone you know is a crack user, you or they will do nothing else but fail or make something fail. You will eventually breakdown or even cause others to breakdown if you don't get help.

Crack will cause you to have a personality disorder. Now ladies, some of you have allowed the enemy to break into your safe place. You have allowed the man drug to force a way into a safe place of yours. Men you have allowed women to do the same thing to you. Now this sex or lust drug can also be extremely addictive. It can cause you to have a personality disorder. You need to know that when you have sex outside a marriage, it can cause a breaking. It can cause a family to break because this person is one who behaves in an uncontrolled and unpredictable way. This sex or lust drug can hit a family hard. These drugs can breakdown a family psychologically. It can also break you down just like the drug called crack.

Now if crack means to breakdown psychologically or cause someone else to breakdown psychologically, then we know that the devil is not playing. The enemy plan is to destroy us. The reason I say that is because if you breakdown psychologically, then that mean that this is relating to the mind or mental processes. In other words, crack affects the mind. Oops, lets pull the covers off the enemy. Let it be known that he is trying with all he got to destroy any and everybody's mind. Not only does it affect the mind of the user, but it also affects the mind of the people close to them. Who is the top dog behind working the mind over? It is Satan, the enemy himself.

The enemy will always suggest thoughts to you. When the enemy begin to interject thoughts in your mind, you must do something. You must cast down the imaginations. You tell yourself, "Self, I am not trying to hear that today, so leave me alone." Sometime you need to tell yourself that you don't want to think about that mess. Do not dwell on the thoughts. Throw them out immediately. If not, it can cause you or your family member to go psycho, which is the root word of psychological. This drug can actually drive you and your family member's crazy if you continue to let the enemy run game on you without getting help. I am sure it will hurt you to see your family member or friend in this state especially if it is your husband or wife.

The sex or lust drug can cause family hearts to be broken into pieces also. Don't continue to let the enemy or this sex drug take you for a ride. And if you took a ride anyway, then tell the enemy that you don't want to ride anymore. Now I don't believe that anyone wants to be a drug addict, but this doesn't stop people from getting addicted. The most commonly asked question is simply how and why? How could my child or parent or spouse become a crack addict, a liar, a thief, a sex or lust addict or someone who cannot be trusted? How could this happen? And why won't they stop? The answer is, the enemy is behind all this. The devil is an angel of the bottomless pit and he wants you to hit rock bottom. Do you get it? Rock bottom! The devil is a liar!

The devil is a murderer and he wants to kill you. He is an old serpent that wants to continue to trick you. He is the prince of demons. He is the prince of this world. He is the ruler of darkness and he never wants you to see the light. He is Satan, the enemy. He is the wicked one so let me tell you what time it is. It is high time to wake up out of sleep and stop getting high off this drug because you have been sleeping with the enemy called crack. You have been sleeping with the enemy called adulterated sex. You have been sleeping with the enemy called lust. You have been sleeping with the enemy called lying and cheating. You have been sleeping with the enemy called gossiping, etc. You have been doing this far too long. You cannot turn a trick into a treat anyway. It is high time to wake up out of darkness. You need to seek God like you never have before. If you don't know, now you know. Don't be afraid to ask for help. Don't be afraid to ask for prayer. We know that the enemy is trying to come in like a flood to drown many families, but guess what? My bible tells me what the Lord will do when the enemy comes in a like a flood.

> *When the enemy shall come in like a*
> *flood, the spirit of the Lord shall lift*
> *up a standard against him.*
> *Isaiah 59: 19*

In other words the Lord shall lift up a rallying point for troops to battle for you. He shall lift up a support base for you. He shall set principles or values that govern the enemy's behavior. So remember this, when the enemy comes in like a flood, or began to apply a lot of pressure to your life with so many storms, then the spirit of the Lord shall appoint a unit of soldiers that are armed and dangerous to go into battle for you! Listen, there are people throughout the nation praying and interceding for you and you don't even know it!

Let us make this prayer nation wide. You that are reading this book right now, I want you to stop and take a moment to pray for every crack addict, every sex addict or any other drug addict and his or her families all across the nation. Make sure that it is at least two or more of you because it will be more effective when you touch and agree. Do it with sincerity. Speak life over each crack addict, each sex addict or any other drug addict and their families. Say that they shall live and not die. Satan I cast you out of every household! I command every foul spirit to get out of your house right now! I speak holiness in your temple. Your breakthrough is coming! I break every negative spirit off of you right now including the lust spirit, sex spirit, lying spirit, manipulating spirit and jezebel spirit.

Remove anything that's not like you Lord God. Speak over your lives as the spirit of the Lord gives it to you. Then just thank Jesus for the victory. Thank you Jesus! Thank you Jesus for lifting up a standard against the enemy. Thank you Jesus for being forgiving. Thank you Jesus for being Alpha and Omega. Thank you for being the beginning and the end. Thank you for being the bread of life. Thank you for being the bright and morning star. Thank you for being a deliverer, yes a deliverer. Thank you for being faithful and true. Thank you for being a great God. Thank you for being the great I Am, the Holy One, the King of Glory, the King of Kings, the Lamb of God, the Life, the Light, the Lord of Lords, the Master, the Prince of Peace, and our Redeemer. Thank you Jesus! Truly you are worthy to be praised!

People don't let the enemy try to drown you or keep you under. You have to be determined that you shall live and not die. You are to also be respected. You are the righteousness of God. In the future, don't let anybody disrespect you by giving you this damaging drug. Believe me, these damaging drugs could be offered to you throughout this life. Yes it may look like you're going to be defeated, but there are unseen forces working for you on your behalf. In all thy getting get an understanding.

Listen, I have experienced drug dealers calling my house. Not only did they call my house but also they called there with threats. Now if this ever happens in your life, it will not set right in your spirit, whether you are saved or not. You can't even begin to understand the sleep that I lost concerning this situation. Now here's someone that is supposed to be close and dear to me telling me not to worry. He is also saying that everything will be all right. OH NO! I don't think so! You must have lost your mind if you think that it will be all right! First of all, I can't tell that everything will be all right when I'm answering threatening phone calls! I don't understand why are they calling in the first place! This issue needs to be fixed. Can somebody help me understand? Especially when they are saying things like, don't let me have to come to your house. This man even stated my address. Yet you say that everything is going to be all right. Not! I don't think so! I don't believe you. On top of that, you put the whole family in danger.

That means that you are out of control and I am not trying to go down with you. Actually I'm thinking that you must be crazy and lost your mind. You just don't put your family in danger like that! Why should I believe you anyway when you have abandoned me? Why should I believe you when you are nowhere to be found? Why should I believe you when you are hiding important information from me? Since I can't sleep, then I might have to rise, take up my bed and walk! I must proceed with caution because I don't know what will happen next. Don't get caught up in situations like this. If you do then make sure that you are in tune with God so that He can guide you. It is crucial to stay rooted and grounded in Gods word. Why? Then you can deal better with issues in your family and everyday lives. When I was dealing with this issue, I was thinking that somebody's mind need to be renewed.

You were created to be Christ like because you are a new man or woman. You should now have a new life. We will please God if we are truly holy. God was created in righteousness. We should walk in righteousness and not messiness. We are supposed to be new creatures in Christ. Now the old man was corrupt. The old man was immoral and dishonest. The old man contained a lot of errors. The old man was contaminated and tainted. The old man was just plain rotten. From the situation here, it looks like I am dealing with an old man syndrome. I even wanted to say, "Hey old man, what is your problem?" "Get it together, or leave me alone." Evidently he needed to be made new again. So when you become a new man then you must change your corrupt conversation. Forsake sin because sin is deceptive. Don't allow the enemy to deceive you with the lust of this world anymore. You were even told that your old foolish desires would destroy you. You must give up all your old bad habits. Return backslider and REPENT! Help us Jesus!

We need to know that all of us are supposed to be part of the same body. I'm speaking of the body of Christ. We need to stop lying to one another and start telling each other the truth. Honesty is important to God. Let me help somebody with something. Even though honesty is important, some of us need to proceed with caution. Why? It is because your abrupt or harsh honesty can wound or hurt someone. There are times when you need to keep your mouth shut. Let me give you an example. If someone is overweight and they say to you, "I am so fat." You don't have to comment and say something like, "You sure are fat." Who even asked you for your two cents anyway? Some of us talk too much. Some of us always have something to say about somebody. If this is you then you need to shut up sometimes. That is a part of your growth process when you have learned how to contain or control your mouth. It took me a long time to learn that one. Every now and then, I almost relapse.

> *Be ye angry, and sin not: let not the*
> *sun go down upon your wrath.*
> *Ephesians 4:26*

Don't ever get so mad that you sin. Some people get so angry that they say, "I need a drink." Do not let your anger cause you to drink alcohol. Do not let your anger cause you to do drugs. You know we mentioned all types of drugs previously. Your drug could be lying or manipulating someone. Now lets get off the drug people. Learn how to forgive. Do not go to bed angry because this will allow the enemy to come on in and activate wickedness. Here is the deal. There is nothing wrong with getting angry but don't stay angry. In other words, you have twenty-four hours to get over it. Trust me, I know that in some cases it is easier said than done, but we must work on it.

> *Neither give place to the devil*
> *Ephesians 4:27*

Don't give the devil a chance. Resist the devil. Don't let the enemy cause a satanic invasion. Remember you must submit unto God first before you can resist the devil. Then he will flee. It is kind of hard to resist the devil when you are sleeping with him. We got to wake up people and see the real deal. We got to stop sleeping with the enemy! You have just gotten lazy I'd say!

Let him that stole steal no more: but
rather let him labor, working with his
hands the thing which is good, that he
may have to give to him that need it.
Ephesians 4:28

If you are a thief, then stop stealing right now! Be honest and work hard legally. You should make an honest living. Selling drugs is not an honest living because you can get locked up for that. So be honest, work hard and never steal anything ever again. Do not even steal a paper clip office worker. Consider your ways. Get it right so you can be able to help someone else that could be facing the same issues.

Let no corrupt communication proceed
out of your mouth, but that which is
good to the use of edifying, that it may
minister grace unto the hearers.
Ephesians 4:29

Stop all your dirty talking. Say the right thing at the right time to help others by what you say. Some people need to be ministered to. So stop speaking evil among one another. Encourage one another to do well. Sow good words to build one another up. Choose your words wisely. Don't make God's spirit sad. Do not sin against the Holy Spirit. Let me make something absolutely clear to you. God will forgive you for all manner of sin and even blasphemy unto men, but the blasphemy against the Holy Ghost will never be forgiven unto men. If you do this then you are in danger of eternal damnation. Those of you, who don't know what blaspheme means, let me tell you. Blasphemy is insulting, cursing, and lacking reverence for God or claim deity.

Let all bitterness, and wrath, and anger
and clamour, and evil speaking, be put
away from you, with all malice.
Ephesians 4:31

Stop being bitter and angry with other people and yourself. Don't yell at one another or cuss each other out. Don't ever be rude. We need to learn how to respect one another. Wow, this is so hard for some people. The reason is because they are so stuck on self. It is all about what I like and what I want. How about being considerate and thoughtful of others. Remember that you reap what you sow. What kind of seeds are you planting? If you are sowing sex with a partner that is not your husband or wife, then remember that a harvest of a baby can come. Choose wisely. If you have been making bad choices due to revenge or just being rebellious, then you should get godly counsel and take heed.

And be ye kind one to another,
tenderhearted, forgiving one another,
even as God for Christ's sake hath
forgiven you. Ephesians 4:32

Be kind and show mercy to one another. Even if things don't go your way, forgive them just as God forgave you. You need to stop holding grudges against other people. Let love be your guide to a healthy life. I choose to love life. I choose to live and not die. I told the devil that his time was up in my household. I refuse to live with my families or my spouse demons operating in my life. The fire was getting too hot so I had to roll out. I had to go. I had to break in order to get my breakthrough. God has got to do a new thing in my life. Help, there is a stranger in the house! Listen, there are some cases when we must show tough love. I know that it is hard to do with a love one but in most cases we must. Don't you ever become a victim of codependency.

Chapter 12
CODEPENDENCY

What is codependency? Codependency is any addictive tendency that keeps us from the center of Gods will. It is an emotional and behavioral condition that affects an individual's ability to have a healthy relationship. People with codependency very often form relationships that are one sided. It is emotionally destructive and abusive. A codependent person does not really live his or her own life. They spend most of their time trying to fix, please, rescue or help the person they may have a relationship with, whether it is a friend, relative or spouse for example. Who does codependency affect? It often affects a spouse, a parent, siblings, friend, family, etc. The person afflicted with an alcohol or drug dependence affects their family and friends. I went to counseling dealing with codependency because the people thought I needed it. I tried but I quit because I knew that nobody could help me but God. A codependent is a person who is in relationship with somebody who is addicted to or controlled by something harmful or destructive. They allow that person's problem to control what they do or how they live their life.

Codependency has broadened to describe anyone from a dysfunctional family. I think that just about hit us all. Dysfunctional families do not acknowledge that problems even exist. As a result, family members learn to block unacceptable or painful impulses, desires, or memories from the mind or conscious. They restrain or hide their feelings and disregard their own needs. They become survivors. They develop behaviors that help them deny, ignore, or avoid difficult emotions. They detach themselves. They don't talk. They don't want to touch the issue. They don't confront the issue. They don't feel and they don't even trust anymore.

Sometimes the codependent person will give all their attention and energy to the family member who is addicted or sick. Now care taking is not always enabling. If there is any care-taking behavior that allows or enables abuse to continue in the family, it needs to be recognized and stopped. The codependent person must identify and embrace his or her feelings and needs. This may include learning to say "No!" You ought to be loving, yet tough sometimes. Hope lies in learning more. The more you understand codependency the better you can cope with its effects.

> *Then Peter and the other apostles*
> *answered and said, We ought to*
> *obey God rather than men.*
> *Acts 5:29*

We need to submit to authority but we need to be free from improper control and manipulation. People who are codependent spend most of their time trying to fix, rescue or help the dependent person when most of the time they don't want to be helped anyway. Listen, we can have compassion for them and want to help them. We can also pray for them all we want, but we can't make somebody love God. We can't make somebody choose God. We have no power to change them. You need to let God change them, but you continue to pray. Each person has to make his or her own choices. You must take a stand to a person that is a controller and a manipulator. A controller and a manipulator are somebody who is trying to run your life to get what they want. You must stand up to a person like that.

If you try to warn your child over and over again about something and they don't listen, then they have to be held responsible for their own mess. They must deal with the choices they continue to make and reap the consequences. How can you tell if a person is controlling you? First of all, if you are in a balanced relationship it is give and take. You cannot always give and never receive. That will not work. That type of relationship can wear you out or drain you if you're not careful. If one person gets their way all the time, then it is control and manipulation. If one person gets their way all the time, then this relationship is out of balance. Some people will actually form their mouth to tell you they love you but yet use you for their own greediness or selfishness.

Listen, anybody can only take so much. Some people even try to manipulate with God and prayers. They may say God told me to tell you to do this when in fact, God never told them to tell you to do any of that. Some people try to put you in a position to make you think you owe them something. Don't ever let a person put you in a position to think you owe them. Why do we let people control and manipulate us anyway? I'll tell you why, it is because of fear, guilt or obligation. We also need to know that some people mistreat others because they have been mistreated.

Now don't mistake godly submission with control and manipulation. There is a difference in godly submission versus control and manipulation. Please listen to me. Don't try to control the Pastor. Pastors please don't try to control your members. Make sure that you hear from God for yourself. We are all made free from anyone's control. So don't try to manipulate or control anybody. Just because I like to work all the time does not mean that you like to work all the time even though work is important. God built us different. We all need to function in our own God giving gifts. Let everybody say, Amen.

Chapter 13
WHO IS THE ENEMY?

*My people are destroyed for the lack of
knowledge: because thou hast rejected
knowledge, I will also reject thee, that thou
shalt be no priest to me: seeing thou hast
forgotten the law (Gods word) of thy God,
I will also forget thy children. Hosea 4: 6*

Listen people, we can be destroyed for not having enough understanding of Gods' word. A lot of times we can get caught up in sinful situations without realizing that it is sin. But sin is destructive no matter how you look at it. So it would be wise and good to get instruction and get an understanding. Gods' word is simply saying that because you rebel or refuse to accept, or believe in His word and be a doer of His word then God will refuse to accept you.

After you receive knowledge or understanding of the word of God then don't just throw it in the trash or out the window and forget about it. If you do, then it will be your own choice to forget about it. God said if you choose to forget His word and what you have learned then He would also forget your children. Now I know you do not want God to forget your children or families now do you? You need to know that if you despise instruction from the word of God then you will be rejected. You will be rejected!

I know some people cannot stand for anybody to tell them what to do. They may say something like, "I am grown, I can do what I want to do." You may be grown in number or age but are you mature and wise in God? It may not be wise to do everything that you want to do even though you have free will or free choice. The reason I say that is because your flesh can get you in a lot of trouble. It is true that you can do whatever you want to do by choice. Whatever you choose to do then I hope you will use godly wisdom with it. Why? The reason is because you will reap the consequences.

Do You Really Know?

When asked the question, "Who is the enemy?" some of you may be saying, "I have plenty of enemies in my life." If I would ask you to name your enemies then some of you would probably name many. You may say my cousin George and his friend Mad Dog. You may say my husband Bill and my sister Regina. You may say my brother Rodney and my wife Brenda. You may say my mom and dad. You may say Ray-Ray and Bunt. You may say my supervisor Jason. You may say my children. You may say my Pastor. You may say my co-worker. You may say my hair stylist, etc. The list could go on and on.

If you believe these people are your enemies then you are way off track. Let's get an understanding right now. What is the correct or appropriate answer, to whom the enemy really is. The enemy is Satan, the adversary, or the devil. The dictionary describes the enemy this way.

1. An unfriendly opponent or somebody who hates and seeks to harm or cause trouble for you. (You need to know that the enemy doesn't like you. He hates you. He always wants to damage or injure you physically,

mentally, morally, emotionally or spiritually). Do you have any so called friends like that? Are you like that? Is your head like that?

2. The enemy is a military opponent, a person or group, especially a military force that fights against another in combat or battle. (Once you have been born again you must know that you have become a soldier for Christ. It is vital that you put on the whole armor of God so that you will become armed and dangerous. There will be warfare. Even though God will or can fight your battles for you, you must know how to fight back yourself because the enemy will launch his attacks when you least expect it. As long as God is on your side then the enemy will be defeated).

3. The enemy is a hostile nation or power. (You need to know what you are dealing with. You are dealing with an angry nation or a group of demonic forces that oppose or hate you for choosing our Lord and Savior Jesus Christ. These demonic forces are assigned to you specifically to break you down). Is there anybody around you constantly trying to break you down or embarrass you? Have you ever had someone shout at you and tell you to shut up while supposedly prophesying to you? You knew that they were angry because of their tone and actions. On top of that they feel as though you can't tell them anything because they know it all. They act like they are the only one that can hear from God. That is not of God. Why do you say that? I say that because God is love and God is kind. The devil is a liar! The devil is hostile and angry. The enemy will always try to cut you down because he knows whom you belong to. Let's pull the covers off the enemy. And the one that profess to be

prophesying with all that anger and hostility, if you listen very closely and carefully they tend to use the word I quite a bit. They may say the spirit said. What spirit are they talking about? They tend not to acknowledge the Lord whatsoever. They try to confuse you by twisting their words. On top of all that, they have a spirit of control and manipulation. These are false prophets. Now a baby Christian may not be able to pick this up in the spirit. Now there is nothing wrong with a prophetic word but you need to know that there are false prophets as well as there are true prophets. I have met some true prophets of God in my lifetime. On the other hand, I have met face to face with some false prophets that came up against me in a mighty way. Psalm 105: 15 reads, "Touch not mine anointed, and do my prophets no harm." God is saying, don't touch mine. Do not touch Gods chosen because God doesn't play that. That means don't touch them by putting your mouth on them or do not hurt them in any way. You are not to damage them, wound them, or injure them. That is a dangerous state to be in. God is concerned for the welfare of His children, so don't touch HIS. Then God says, and do MY prophets no harm. You better not harm Gods prophets either because that will put you in a dangerous state also. Do not damage them, wound them, or injure them in anyway shape or form. You and I would be wise to take heed to this! So be very careful not to open your mouth against Gods anointed or Gods prophets.

4. The enemy will be something that harms or opposes you. (The enemy is against what you stand for so he will try to hurt you in many ways. The enemy will influence someone to put you down, talk about you,

abuse you, disrespect you, confuse you, misunderstand you, misuse you, control you and manipulate you. There will always be conflict when their way of living are in opposition from yours. This is why you cannot partner up with anybody. This is why you cannot fellowship with anybody). For instance, if you choose to marry someone who does not believe in God, but yet you believe in God, then you should and must expect conflict. There will be a lot of conflict because you started out in opposition. You need to know that this type of relationship can cause you a lot of heartache and pain. Relationships like this can harm you physically, mentally, emotionally and spiritually. Be very careful when you choose.

Now Satan can use anybody. Let me name a few. Satan can use your husband. He can use your wife. He can use your brother or sister. He can use your parents. He can use your children. He can use your Pastor. He can use your teacher. He can use your family and friends. He can use your supervisor and co-workers. The enemy can also use you and me. Now these people are not the enemy (Satan), but the source from which they may be operating is the enemy.

Chapter 14
I. WHAT IS THE ENEMY'S INTENTION?

A.   The enemy wants to undo Gods' work.

> *They on the rock are they, which, when*
> *they hear, receive the word with joy;*
> *and these have no root, which for a*
> *while believe, and in time of temptation*
> *fall away. Luke 8: 13 (KJV)*

> *The seeds that fell on rocky ground are*
> *the people who gladly hear the message*
> *(Gods' word) and accept it. But they*
> *don't have deep roots, and they believe*
> *only for a little while. As soon as life*
> *gets hard, they give up. Luke 8: 13 (CEV)*

This is the parable of the sower. The seed is the word of God. This scripture is simply speaking about unstable (rocky), emotional hearers (You may jump up and down, clap your hands, dance and stump your feet. You may speak in tongues and read your bible everyday of the week. You may read at home, work or even cry concerning the message) but as soon as the enemy tempts you with words or compliments, then you simply yield yourself to temptation. As soon as you walk out the church or get off work and get into your car, you may start cussing somebody out. You may even turn into a very promiscuous person. Some people don't even wait. They may do it right there in the church or even at work. This is exactly what the enemy wants you to do. The enemy doesn't mind you having a good time in church but as soon as you leave church here is what happens. After church is over, then Satan tempts you. You will fall away if you are not rooted and grounded in the word of God. You will yield to temptation. Trust me, you are not fooling anybody but yourself.

The enemy will steal your joy, your peace, your children, your spouse, your friends, your job, your finances, your house, your virginity, etc. Why? It is because his intentions are to undo Gods' work! So don't you dare go along with sleeping with that man or woman just because you believe you are going to marry him or her. Don't you dare sleep with him or her because somebody told you that in Gods eye you are still married to him or her when in fact you are not. The devil is a liar! Don't you let anybody even feed you that mess! It is a trick of the enemy! Don't you dare sleep with him or her due to a prophecy or a dream that you had. That prophecy could be true for the future, but you may be getting ahead of yourself. Wait on God because the prophecy that you received could be a proph-a-lie.

The enemy has a purpose in mind for you. He has a plan that he wants to achieve. The enemy's plan is to stop you from reaching your destiny. His intentions are to hurt you in anyway possible so that you can give up and let go of God. The enemy comes to kill, steal, and destroy. God came that you might have life and that more abundantly. The enemy definitely doesn't want you to understand this. He hates it when you have joy. He hates it when you have peace.

Let me give you an example of how the enemy will steal your joy and peace. You could be working on your job with much joy, oh but the devil doesn't like that. In this case, the enemy may use a supervisor or co-worker to come against you to kill, steal or even destroy your joy. Sometimes they don't even have a clue that Satan (the enemy) is using them. I have had that happen to me even with my family. Believe me, the enemy will find someone who doesn't mind being influenced by him. Remember they are not the enemy but can be greatly influenced by the enemy.

Even though they are not the enemy, we sometimes feel the need to snap, crackle and pop (slang for go off on them or give them a piece of your mind). Some of us may even want to beat them down, okay? If this is you, then all I can say is been there, done that. But that is the wrong approach. The reason I say that is because we are not fighting against flesh and blood here. There is a war going on.

There is a huge war going on against marriages. The enemy is sowing seed that could kill the purpose of God in our marriages. We need marriages that overcome the enemy. We need marriages that have a solid rock foundation. Now we all know that there are no perfect marriages but some are not meant to be even though you try to work it. Some marriages are like a house that was built on sand. When the storm comes it withers away. In some cases the storm never stops because of the evil influence.

> *Ephesians 6: 12-13*
> *For we wrestle not against flesh and blood,*
> *but against principalities, against powers,*
> *against the rulers of darkness of this world,*
> *against spiritual wickedness in high places.*
> *(verse 12)*

I. WHAT IS THE ENEMY INTENTIONS

Wherefore take unto you the whole armour
of God, that ye may be able to withstand in
the evil day, and having done all, to stand.
(verse 13)

We are not fighting a physical fight but there is a war going on and if you want to win you better make sure you and your head got Jesus deep within. There is a spiritual warfare going on. Kingdoms exist that we don't see with the natural eye. The scripture states that we are fighting against principalities. Principalities are rulers and governments. There are principalities that have an assignment against your destiny even though you could have nations locked up in your wound. A principality is a territory ruled by a prince. Now there is an order of different ranks with the demonic forces. A prince ranks highly in their field. The prince of this world is Satan (the enemy).

We are fighting against powers. The powers this scripture is speaking of is control and influence. The enemy uses powers to control and influence people and their actions. The enemy uses powers to influence political control. The enemy uses powers to govern political or financial power. There is power to persuade. It is the ability to influence people judgements or emotions.

We are fighting against the rulers of darkness of this world. Satan (the enemy) rules the darkness. Satan governs and exercises authority over darkness. What is darkness? Darkness means that there is absence of light. Darkness also shows a sign of ignorance or being unlearned. Whenever there is darkness affliction is present. Whenever there is darkness disobedience is present. If light marries darkness then affliction will be present on a regular basis. When we speak of darkness with Satan being the ruler, then we are speaking of a nightfall. Night is the time between somebody's going to sleep and hopefully waking in the morning. It is an absence of light. It is the absence of consciousness. It is the absence of enlightenment. Night is a period marked by grief, gloom, ignorance, or obscurity. We ought to be very careful not to walk in disobedience or darkness. The reason I say that is because we might fall and trip over something. Darkness causes you to fall. By the way, we call that nightfall.

Listen, there is a real hell that is a place of torment. If you continue to walk in outer darkness then there will be everlasting punishment. There will be everlasting destruction. There will be everlasting fire and that is the lake of fire. Who is hell prepared for? Hell is prepared for the devil and his angels. Hell is prepared for the wicked. Hell is prepared for the disobedient. Hell is prepared for the fallen angels. Hell is prepared for the beast and the false prophet. Hell is prepared for the worshippers of the beast. Hell is prepared for the rejecters of the Gospel, which is the word of God.

We are fighting against spiritual wickedness in high places. Wickedness is dangerous. Wickedness is capable of causing harm to you. Wickedness will cause you discomfort, distress, or disappointment. It is disgusting and it even tastes and smells disgusting. It is also repulsive (very unpleasant). Wickedness makes somebody feel disgust and it makes somebody feel a very strong dislike. In other words, they don't have to tell you that they dislike you because you will feel it very strongly. Wicked people are bad people. These are people who do very bad things. Wicked people will cuss God out, the Pastor out and you out also. We are talking about spiritual wickedness in high places. The high places are positions of power, authority or influence. Remember that even though the enemy has power, God gave us wide dominion. That means that we have authority to govern and delegate by God. The reason I say that is because we are under Gods control and dominion is secured by His resurrection.

That means that we are higher than the enemy. That means that the enemy may try his influence but it won't work. He may try to control or manipulate us but it won't work. He may try to govern or control our finances but it won't work. He may try to govern or control our judgement or emotions but it won't work. Why? The reason is because we have authority to govern the enemy. God gave us power over the enemy. God gave us authority and when God gives you authority every system has to serve you. So there is no reason that your finances should be locked up because it got to serve you.

Now sometimes we can go to work with no challenges. We can go to school with no challenges. We can go to church with no challenges. We can go home with no challenges. Then all of a sudden the enemy attacks you with evil. The evil day came that verse thirteen was talking about. You need to do all you can to stand against the evil day without going over the edge. You need to know that we are not fighting against humans here. We are fighting against forces and against rulers of darkness and powers in the spiritual realm.

Listen, the enemy governs the darkness because he is the ruler of darkness. We are dealing with spiritual wickedness in high places. The enemy makes up the rules of the games being played. The enemy wants to guide your behavior or actions. Since the enemy governs the darkness then that means that he exercises a controlling authority over you while you are walking in darkness. If you let him control you, then he will keep you blind and living in darkness. He will keep you in sleep mode. Don't let the enemy have any control over your life. Submit to God and resist the devil.

The enemy wants you to get drunk off of the world's way of doing things so that your vision will be blurred. If your vision is blurred then you cannot see clearly. In other words, the enemy wants to keep you in sleep mode. You must not leave your home without proper attire. You must have on the whole armor of God. Do not miss one stitch. I am sure most of us had to face an evil day at one time or another. No, we didn't like it. I'm sure it was an unpleasant day. It was a hurtful day. It was a harmful day. It was a painful day and maybe even an upsetting day. But we made it through somehow. Let's give God the praise for that! Thank you Jesus!

Give thanks to our Lord and Savior Jesus Christ. Sure you may have been treated wrongly and it didn't feel good. But don't fall away from all that God taught you in His word. Don't give up or give into the enemy devices. When you have done all you can do just stand. Stand through the storm. Stand through the pain. Stand through the hurt. Even if you have to cry sometime, go ahead and cry.

> *Weeping may endure for a night, but*
> *joy cometh in the morning.*
> *Psalms 30: 5*

Joy is promised to us from God Almighty! We need to learn to stand on Gods' promises and be sure to wear the whole armor of God. Don't be moved by what the enemy throws at you to get you off track. Do all you can do to stand. Give it your all and don't give in. Don't give up. When you have on the whole armor of God, then you are armed and dangerous. Why do you say that? I say that because with your armor you will be equipped with weapons. You need weapons to fight the enemy. Your armor is a defensive covering used in battle.

I. WHAT IS THE ENEMY INTENTIONS

It will be wise to stay covered because the attacks will come. They will come when you least expect it. Let us find out what armor should we be prepared to wear each and everyday.

Since you are a soldier for Christ, then you need to learn how to fight. Stop sitting around taking all those low blows that the devil is dishing out to you. You can do something about it since you have become a soldier in the army. The problem for some is that they have not enlisted yet in the Christian Army. If you have not enlisted in the Christian Army today, then you need to do so as soon as possible (ASAP). The reason I say that is because if you try to apply these principles and you are not a part of the winning team, then it will not work for you. Why do you say that? I say that because how can you fight the enemy when you are partners with the enemy? You need to be covered by God. The armor that God expects us to wear is a defensive covering used in battle. I am saying that to say this, you will have battles. You will have to fight so why not get equipped.

Chapter 15
THE SOLDIERS EQUIPMENT

Ephesians 6: 14-17
Stand therefore, having your loins girt
about with truth, and having on the
breastplate of righteousness; (verse 14)

There are three things stated in this scripture that you must wear everyday. It is a part of your armor. Those three things are (1) Standing power, (2) You need to have a truth quality and (3) You must have on the breastplate of righteousness.

First, you should stand upright in God. Stand on His promises. That is your standing power. You must stand against the wiles (trickery, guile, deceitful and cunning) of the devil, but you must have on the whole armor of God. Since you are the righteousness of God, you must take a stand and don't allow anyone to put you in a sitting or lying position. The reason I say that is because you don't know what may come up against you next. Have you ever been a victim of a fight and someone came charging at you suddenly while you were sitting down? You saw them coming even though you were in a sitting position. Maybe you were too comfortable. There are times when you need to come out of your comfort zone. You don't just sit there and let them get the best of you now do you? No! You stand up so you can be ready for the attack. You have to stand and protect yourself. As long as you are standing upright in God then you are sure to be covered and protected. Make sure that you have an insurance policy to be protected from any unexpected attacks. Let God cover you, protect you, insure you, or even hide you in a time of trouble. Let Him be your shelter from bad weather. Let God be your defense.

Secondly, you need to have on a truth quality. You should have on honesty, sincerity and integrity. You must also be equipped with loyalty. Gird up your loins means to prepare and strengthen yourself to do something that could be difficult and challenging. Why? It is because you are going to need some support. You need to know that it will not always be easy. There are going to be some difficult times in your life. Perhaps the difficult times may be with finances, sickness and disease, disappointments, trauma, etc. How many of you are honest and sincere about your finances. How truthful are you about your taxes? Are you walking in integrity when it comes to making an honest living? There may be difficult times even in your relationships.

How honest are you in your relationships? Do you have on a truth quality? How loyal are you with your spouse? When there is dishonesty and disrespect in a relationship that is not a good sign. It will cause what was a good relationship to go bad. If this happens, then there may be disappointments, domestic violence, abuse, divorce, etc. Be sincere and honest about it. Be a person of integrity. God is truth so stay loyal and faithful to God no matter what you go through. Don't let anyone cause you to walk in dishonesty or disobedience. Be a man or woman of integrity.

Finally, you need to have on the breastplate of righteousness. Why is it so important to have on the breastplate of righteousness? The breastplate is a defensive armor for the breast and soldiers wear it. Your breast is where your emotions sit. It is the seat of emotions. It is the place where human emotions reside. If someone hurts you or you lose a loved one don't let it become your seat of emotions. Now if you continue to sit there in that emotion for a long period of time then it can cause damage to your health. Now when someone hurts you or you lose a loved one, then don't let people tell you to just get over it. Sometimes you have to cry to keep from going crazy or losing your mind. After you have cried about it then there is a healing process that you must go through. It is all right to cry. The bible states that Jesus wept.

Please don't stay in the position of sitting in your emotions forever because there are other people that need you. The emotions are weapons for the enemy. If you do stay in that position, then you will not be able to be used for the Kingdom of God. You must remember that joy is coming in the morning but you got to hold on. Remember that the joy of the Lord is your strength! Get your strength back!

Get help if you must but don't just stay there being easily swayed by your emotions forever. Don't be so easily affected by what someone say or do to you. Don't let them agitate or disturb you so easily. When you sit you are considered to be in a riders position. Some people will take you for a ride. Of course this can or will hurt you but you must face your difficulties or challenges boldly. Hold on, a change is going to come. You must develop what I call thick skin.

Have you armed yourself with the word of God? Bold speech does not come from an empty heart but bold speech comes from much word of God. It is a natural thing to have feelings and reactions to certain emotions such as disappointments. If someone disappoints you it is natural for you to feel hurt or emotional or even react to this emotion. That's why we are to be prepared and make sure that we are armed. Some of us have dealt with domestic violence, divorce, tragedy, heartache and pain but yet we can't seem to get through the pain. This may occur if we don't equip ourselves with the whole armor of God.

Arm yourself with the word of God. This will be healthy for you. The breast has a lot to do with your health. The breast is an organ on a human chest. A lot of times we feel the need to get things off our chest due to guilt, worry, disappointments, being angry or maybe even being embarrassed. In those cases, we especially feel the need to talk about it. Talking about it may reduce or remove some of the feelings we are having. Be careful whom you confide in or release your emotions to. Why do you say that? The reason I say that is because the emotions are weapons for the enemy. Can you trust the person that you confide in?

To stay healthy we must eat right and normally your food is served on a plate. Let's choose healthy choices. What are you allowing yourself to be fed? What are you letting people serve you on your plate? Can your heart take it? A plate is a household dish. What kind of dishes are people bringing to your house? Who are you inviting to your house? What are people feeding you when you go to their house? Is it good food or is it bad food? What kind of dishes are they bringing to your house? Are you allowing people to dish out unhealthy food to you? Have you allowed someone to put a hold on you in your own house? Please don't let anyone put you in bondage or prison in your own home. Don't allow them to put you in bondage or prison in their own home either.

If you are allowing a portion of abuse to be put on your plate, whether it is mental, physical or emotional then stop eating it. If you allowed domestic violence to be put on your plate then stop eating it. There are some conversations you need to leave off your plate also. You need to know that you can make it because you are not alone. You are not alone. God will be with you and He will see to it that you make it but you got to stand when it gets rough. You don't have to continue to eat food that is hazardous to your health. You must get rid of the unhealthy food that you chose in the first place. You must get rid of the unhealthy food that has been served to you on your plate because you will gain a lot of unnecessary weight. You do not need all that weight! It is too fattening! It will literally drain you and possibly kill you, so be very careful of your surroundings.

> *And your feet shod with the preparation*
> *of the gospel of peace; Ephesians 6: 15*

Now the scripture states and your feet shod. Shod is the past tense of shoe. Shod is your footgear. Normally when you put your shoes on you begin to walk. My question to you is, "How are you walking?" Your shoes are used as a protective covering but some of us are not wearing the right shoes to be covered. "What kind of shoes have you been wearing?" "What kind of footgear are you wearing right now?"

Loafer Shoes:

Maybe you have been wearing loafers too much. A loafer is a lazy unconcerned person who avoids work and wastes time. You will find in most cases that if you do not work you will not eat. If you do not work to study the word of God then you will not eat properly. If you do not work on pleasing God rather than pleasing people then you will not eat properly. Forget about what your neighbor said about you. Forget about what auntie Shirley said about you and continue to please God. Do you avoid doing the work of God? Are you unconcerned about God? Do you waste time instead of studying the word of God? Sometimes you need to get on your face and have a little talk with Jesus. In some cases you may need to turn the phone off so that you will not be distracted.

2Timothy 2: 15 states that you need to, "study to show thyself approved unto God, a workman that needeth not to be ashamed, rightly dividing the word of truth." Do you believe everything you hear? Don't be ashamed of Gods' word. Don't be ashamed to check someone's teachings. Don't be ashamed to be God's workman. The more you study the word of God, the more you will be able to divide the word. You will begin to know what is true and what is false. God also wants you to study for yourself. Why? The reason is because there are hidden treasures in the word. How can you find the gold or the hidden treasures unless you search for it. You must search the scriptures. To study means to learn about by reading and searching. God wants you to read and search the scriptures for more understanding. We have too many people that are unlearned. In all thy getting, get an understanding. As you begin to work and do the will of God then God can work on you to build character. Remember that the work that you do in God is designed for Gods' Glory. You are divinely called to do a work so stop being so lazy. You need to stop loafing around before you become penniless. Stop walking around and hanging out with those penny loafers. You need to connect with somebody that is going somewhere. If this is you wearing those lazy loafers, then you need to change your shoes please. Change shoes! Change shoes!

Mule Shoes:

Maybe you have been wearing the mule shoe too much. A mule is a very stubborn person. You won't bend and you are stiff. You will not change for anybody even though you should change some of your ways. You think your way is the best way all the time. You are hard headed. You want to have it your way and not Gods' way. God is not Burger King! Not only do you want it your way but you also get angry when others disagree with you. You believe that they are against you. You are so stubborn that you become controlling. Maybe you are difficult to deal with because you are stuck in tradition. Maybe you are saying, "Well, that's the way I was raised and that's just how I am." Just because you were raised that way does not make it right. Do you rebel against everything God wants you to do? Maybe you are afraid to step out of your comfort zone. Do you think too highly of yourself and rebel against God? If this is you then you are dealing with witchcraft. If this is you wearing the mule shoe then you won't bend at all. You also tend to be kind of hard on people that you can't control. So please change shoes. Change shoes! Change shoes!

Clog Shoes:

Maybe you have been wearing the clog shoe too much. A clog is something or somebody that works against somebody as an obstacle or hindrance. This shoe is known for making a lot of noise. If you wear this type of shoe then you are blocking someone with dirt and mess because you talk too much. Oh boy, you never shut up! Your ears are clogged up and you are dull in hearing. Stop putting all your business and other people business in the streets. This happens because of all the mess you have allowed in your life. It is now starting to creep into your life. Creep, creep, creep, creep. Stop creeping! Are you an obstacle in somebody's way? Are you a hindrance to someone? Are you trying to hold somebody back? You know that clogs make a lot of noise. Are you making a lot of unnecessary noise? Are you talking loud and saying nothing?

Are you the one clogging people up with junk? What are your conversations like at the workplace? What are your conversations like at home? How many faces do you smile in but yet stab them in the back?

Maybe you just spoke with somebody on the phone. After you hung up with them you rushed to call somebody else to talk about them. If this is you then you are clogging their ears up with junk. Take those clogs off because your feet are getting dusty, with your little dusty self. Some people feet are so dusty that they stink. I remember when I used to go to the clubs. I used to talk about any and everybody. My feet became very dusty from talking about people so much. I had the whole club stinking! Some of you have kicked up so much dust wearing those clog shoes yourself. You have clogged up the eyesight of other people. If you are the one that is wearing this type of shoe, then you need to change your shoes. Change shoes! Change shoes!

Barefooted:

Are you walking around barefooted? If this is you then you are walking around with no protection at all. You are like a person that is walking around having unprotected sex. It is like riding in a car without your seatbelt. The reason being is because you are not planted in God. You are without preparation. You are without understanding. You are without salvation. You are also easily offended. You are considered to be simple. It would be nothing for you to expose yourself because you will do anything, you will say anything and go anywhere. It is as simple as that. Proverbs 25:19 reads, "Confidence in an unfaithful man in time of trouble is like a broken tooth, and a foot out of joint." Listen, it is unwise to put your faith in an unfaithful man. Proverbs 14:15 reads, "The simple believes every word: but the prudent man looks well to his going." In other words, don't be stupid and believe all that you hear. A prudent or wise man knows where he is headed and he or she looks for credibility in a person. Are they believable and easy to believe? Are they trustworthy by inspiring trust and confidence? If he or she is credible then this is military effective of sufficient strength to function effectively. If a person is credible in a marriage then this is military effective. This alone can give you sufficient strength to function effectively.

Only the most credulous person will readily believe an outrageous lie. Don't be so gullible and too easily convinced that something is always true. If he or she cannot be trusted then he or she will not support your weight. If this is you, then you need to get yourself some protection quick! Get shoes! Get shoes!

Combat boots:

Do you have your boots on? I am not talking about any boots. I am talking about your combat boots. These are heavy boots. When you have your combat boots on, then you are prepared and ready for warfare. These boots may be heavy because the warfare may get heavy. Tell the enemy, "These boots are made for walking and I'll walk all over you!" Luke 10:19 reads, "Behold, I give unto you power to tread (to walk on or walk over) on serpents and scorpions and over all the power of the enemy: and nothing shall by any means hurt you." Listen, God gave us power over all the powers of the enemy. Then the scripture says, and nothing shall by any means hurt you. While I was meditating on this scripture, I thought to myself. I was hurt in my past relationships, so what happened? I realize now that I was not wearing the right shoes. As long as you have your combat boots on, you can walk on or over serpents. Whatever they dish out will not hurt you. I am speaking of people who are snakes. They are sly and treacherous people. They could be charming and yet poisonous people. You don't need that in your life. So why not walk on or walk over this type of spirit because God gave you the enabling power to do so.

As long as you have your combat boots on you will be able to walk on or walk over scorpions also and not get hurt. A scorpion will sting you. This type of person will do things to you to cause a sharp pain. You will become wounded because of the sting. The sting can hurt you and sometimes it will cause you to swell. Do not take matters in your own hands by letting the flesh swell. Control your actions. You know how we swell up sometimes and be ready to fight physically.

A sting hurts. Has a bee ever stung you? Continue to stay in the presence of God and I am sure the swelling will go down in a couple of days.

Now there are different methods of an attack. The first attack I'd like to mention is the ambush takeover due to the need of an ambush makeover. Listen, the enemy will try to take over your life and control or influence everything that you do. In some cases you will submit to the enemy. A lot of times this happens due to the fact that God need to make us over. We must allow God to make us over. We should be submitting to God and resisting the devil (the enemy). The only way we can resist the enemy is to allow God to equip us with the necessary attire.

Secondly I'd like to mention the surprise attack. What is a surprise? Surprise means to take somebody or something unaware. Maybe the enemy surprisingly began to take or influence your sister or brother. Maybe the enemy surprisingly took your husband or wife. Maybe the enemy took your house, your car, your finances and your children. All of this could have come as a surprise to you. When somebody surprises you then that means that you will get something unexpectedly. Maybe the enemy struck you with an infirmity or sickness like high blood pressure or diabetes and it came upon you unexpectedly. Listen, surprise attacks are nothing nice. A surprise also means to trick somebody or to cause somebody to do something unexpected by trickery or deceit.

Finally I'd like to mention the personal combat for champions. What is a champion? A champion is a victor in battle. A champion is a person that competes in a battle and wins the tournament. He or she is a defender. God defends, supports, or promotes you in rank. A champion is a remarkable person. He or she is somebody who exemplifies excellence

161

or achievement. He or she is a warrior. This particular person fights for what they stand for and believe in. I believe in my Lord and Savior Jesus Christ. Hallelujah! Oh but somebody better watch out for the battle cry. This is when the soldiers shout and cry out to God for help or support. It is an encouraging shout or cry that soldiers make before going into battle. The combat boots are good to wear for protection just in case you might have to kick something or someone. Maybe you want to kick the habit of chasing prophecies, smoking, alcohol, drugs, gossiping, controlling, manipulation, lying, backbiting, fornicating, etc. Maybe you want to kick the habit of being in an abusive relationship. You must walk in the spirit, then you shall not fulfill the lust of the flesh. Wear shoes! Wear shoes!

Running Shoes:

Now this last particular shoe I am going to mention is called the running shoe. This particular shoe brings about exercise, flowing continuously, and advancing. When you think of running you should think of striving. I'm speaking of striving spiritually. You ought to be working out one's salvation. I Corinthians 9: 24 reads, "Know ye not that they which run in a race run all, but one receives the prize? So run that you may obtain the prize." In other words, you know that many runners enter a race, and only one of them wins the prize. In this case we all can run to win! Athletes run hard to win a crown. We as believers run for a crown that will last forever.

Before you begin to run you must prepare yourself. When you start this exercise you don't just start out running. You must prepare yourself because you can get hurt in the process. You must be ready. Be ready in advance for future events.

You must be equipped with the necessary shoes to run in. You must study and do your homework because you will have an exam or test.

Prepare yourself for the lessons to come. Prepare yourself with the gospel of peace. The gospel is the teachings of Jesus Christ. The gospel is Gods word. You must study Gods word because you will be tested. You will find out how much word you have when it comes down to understanding peace. Do you have the right footgear on to walk in peace? Prepare to exercise before you begin to run. This may be the time that you must do some stretching. Trust me, you will be stretched sometimes in your life. Wear shoes! Wear shoes!

What is peace, since your feet should be shod with the preparation of the gospel of peace? Peace is the state of harmony and unity. Peace is the presence and experience of right relationships. Your source of peace is God, Christ and the Holy Spirit. You will not have peace if you are in a relationship with the wicked. Why? The wicked do not know anything about peace.

> *The way of peace they know not, and*
> *there is no judgement in their goings:*
> *they have made them crooked paths:*
> *whosoever goeth therein shall not know*
> *peace. Isaiah 59: 8*

> *There is no peace, saith the Lord, unto*
> *the wicked. Isaiah 48: 22*

The wicked do not know peace because of spiritual ignorance. There will be injustice towards you meaning that they will treat you unfair. There will be unjust treatment. There will be crookedness meaning that they are twisted, often in more than one place or area of their lives. When they are crooked it also means that they are not legal. They are illegal and dishonest. They will not abide by the rules of God. Take a good look at the picture of your life right now. Some of your relationships are very crooked and are not aligned properly. Why? It is because of their evil ways, there will be no peace. So remember, if you decide to enter into a relationship like this, then you shall not have peace and you will always be restless.

God commands you to depart from evil and seek peace. This could be good for you. Sometimes you just might have to say farewell to a wrong relationship. Finally my brother, I have to say good-bye because I am striving for perfection. I need some good and pure comfort. I need someone who is in unity with my mind in Christ Jesus so that I may live in peace because God is a God of peace. You might have to put it away from you because when you enter into marriage ladies, you are to marry a king. Kings will lead you into a quiet and peaceable life without all that lying, cheating and wickedness. Lying lips are an abomination to the Lord anyway. Now I know you don't want to be a part of that do you?

> *Depart from evil, and do good; seek peace*
> *and pursue it. Psalms 34: 14*

> *Finally, brethren, farewell. Be perfect, be*
> *of good comfort, be of one mind, live in*
> *peace, and the God of love and peace shall*
> *be with you. 2 Corinthians 13: 11*

> *Let all bitterness, and wrath, and anger,*
> *and clamour, and evil speaking, be put*
> *away from you, with all malice:*
> *Ephesians 4: 31*

Make sure before you try to minister or witness to anyone that you have on the right shoes. Make sure you study and prepare yourself for what is to come. Make sure you are prepared with the gospel of peace. Peace is one of the fruit of the spirit. Walk in the spirit, and you shall not fulfill the lust of the flesh. Luke 1: 79 reads, "To give light to them that sit in darkness and in the shadow of death, to guide our feet into the way of peace." Let God guide you the right way. Roman 8: 6 reads, "For to be carnally minded is death, but to be spiritually minded is life and peace." As long as you are spiritually minded, then there will be life and peace. On the other hand, to be carnal or operating out of your flesh shows a sign of spiritual death. Now lets continue with the armor of God.

> *Above all, taking the shield of faith,*
> *wherewith ye shall be able to quench*
> *all the fiery darts of the wicked.*
> *Ephesians 6: 16*

Above all meaning give this your highest respect. Let your faith be your shield. Without faith it is impossible to please God. It is very important to have faith. Let your trust in God be your shield. Let your belief and devotion to God be your shield. Let your loyalty to God be your shield and do not waiver. Keep your faith in God because God is faithful and just to do what He said that He would do. Stand on His promises. Now some of us have been faithful to a dead thing and it is high time for you to wake up and get your breakthrough. God is not dead but He is yet alive! I am here to tell you that God can deliver you from a dead situation. Stay loyal and faithful to God and let God be your shield. What is a shield? A shield is a piece of armor carried on the arm and used as a protection against weapons, blows, arrows, bullets, and projectiles. What is a weapon? A weapon is a device used to injure or kill an opponent. A weapon is something used to gain advantage.

The enemy doesn't like you so this is why you should be armed at all times just in case there is a sudden attack. Maybe you are trusting God for something that seem impossible. Maybe you are the one with that crazy type of faith. Well there seem to always be someone around you that don't believe. The enemy sends them to cut you down or act like you are crazy. Just keep believing anyway because they don't have a clue what God can do! When the sudden attack comes, it could blow you away unless you have your shield of faith on for safety.

The core meaning of using a shield is to keep safe from actual or potential injury, danger, or attack. As long as you are wearing the shield of faith then you shall be able to quench or to extinguish everything the enemy sends your way. The adversity or issues of life will try your faith. You need to know that the wicked will persecute you and he will try to bring up your past. The enemy loves to have you burning mad. The enemy wants you to get angry enough to burn in lust, burn in disrespect, burn in violence, burn in abuse, burn in trauma, etc. You must know how to put the fire out by using a fire extinguisher. This will bring all the mess to an end. It will also eliminate its effects. Put out those things that the wicked caused you to get so very angry about, to the point of burning up. You must put it out! This is highly important. It must come to an end. You must kill that situation completely. Destroy it! Let it go!

Maybe it was once valid in your life but now it is no longer valid. Maybe it was once applicable for you but now it is no longer applicable for you, so kill it and let it go. You must eliminate the effects that it once had on your life. Keep your shield on baby! Keep believing and trusting God for your breakthrough. The enemy will use darts to throw at you as if he's playing a game. He does not want you to make it. Darts are deadly and destructive weapons. These darts will cause severe afflictions. There will be bitter words. There will be slanderous tongues. There will be false witnesses. All these things can cause you to fall from the hand of God. This could also cause you to be broken. The enemy will always try to run a game on you. The enemy is full of games and he will always try to burn you.

The enemy will always throw blows at you. He will throw low blows and cold blows. He loves to drop a bomb on you. The enemy uses these darts as a weapon to slow you down or even stop you from reaching your destiny. When darts are used, its movement is a sudden one. So there will be sudden attacks. He definitely doesn't want you to keep your faith or trust in God. No matter how much he tries to burn you or bring your past up, stay loyal to God. You must stay focused and believe God no matter what the situation looks like. Tell the enemy that you got a future ahead of you.

> *And take the helmet of salvation, and the*
> *sword of the Spirit, which is the word of*
> *God. Ephesians 6: 17*

You must also wear your helmet. This is the armor for your head. It is worn on your head for protection. Helm is the root word of helmet. It means position of control. It is a position of leadership. Who is the head of your life? Is your head covering you? Maybe the enemy used to be your head but now there is a new Sheriff in town. His name is Jesus Christ. Now you have a new way of living. You are a new creature in Christ. You need to have your mind made up that you are going to serve God and let God be the head of your life. The question is who is the head of your life? Who is in control of your life? Let our Lord and Savior Jesus Christ control what you say, what you do and where you go. Your helmet must be made up of two things. First salvation, in which this could keep you from harm, destruction, difficulty, or failure. Salvation is deliverance from sin through Jesus Christ. Is your head covering you or is he causing you harm, destruction, difficulty or failure? Secondly, your helmet should have the sword of the spirit. A sword is a weapon of war. A sword is Gods word. The spirit is Gods agency. The spirit of God should be the controlling influence. What spirit is influencing you today? What spirit is controlling your head toady? Is the spirit of God the controlling influence? The helmet should consist of the word of God. The word of God is communication from God to man within the scriptures. Being in Gods word, being a doer and a believer will give you several good things. 1) It will give you a standard of conduct. 2) It will give you restraints. 3) It will guide you. 4) It will give you a source of joy. 5) It will give you a source of new life. 6) It will give you spiritual food. 7) It will give you character. Listen, it is not enough just to read the word of God. You should be a doer and a believer of the word of God. Your head should be a believer and a doer of the word of God. So be sure to wear your helmet for protection.

You must realize that Satan (the enemy) is deliberately committing himself to a plan to destroy you. He is determined and focused on that one thing to destroy you or hurt you tremendously to the point of no return. For instance, someone may be out of church right now because someone hurt or offended him or her in the church. They prefer to teach themselves at home, on his or her own, without fellowship, without submitting, without serving, without accountability, without giving and without forgiving. This is an excuse and a trick by your soon to be partner, Satan, if you keep believing that. Honey, don't get it wrong. The devil goes to church to but don't let that keep you from fellowship.

Now there is nothing wrong with studying at home because the bible clearly states that you should study. I can't think of a better place other than church that you should study. You must study to show thyself approved. You should study. Let me make something clear to you. Hebrew 10:25 reads, "Do not forsake the assembling of ourselves together..." Church attendance is important. We all need guidance. No one is exempt. The absence of spiritual leadership can cause you to backslide. You need accountability in your decision making. You need to receive wise counsel. Ask God to put people in your life that will hold you accountable. Don't be surrounded by bad counsel. If you surround yourself around wise counsel then they may be able to determine by God your greed, your lust, your anger, etc., and be able to help you to make better decisions.

If you are not rooted and grounded in Gods word, then this could cause you to backslide. Pride itself can cause you to backslide. Pride comes before destruction and a haughty spirit before a fall. You can love the world so much that it can even cause you to backslide. Backsliding is simply turning away from God after you have been converted. Some of us have made up in our minds that we didn't turn our back on God, but we were just getting away from the people. Been there done that! This is how the enemy puts you in a dangerous state. If you stay in this state then you will eventually get weak. Listen, I repeat, this is a very dangerous state to be in!

The enemy wants you to give up on God. He wants you to think you are weak to even be a Christian. The enemy wants you to think that you are not hard but yet you are a square if you are a true Christian. It's just a trick of the enemy. I am not falling for that trick and you shouldn't either.

Chapter 16
II. WHAT IS THE ENEMY'S INTENTION?

B. To make men and women turn away from God.

Job 2: 1-10 (The story of Job)

In the story of Job, he loses his health because of Satan (the enemy). Jobs' wife told him to curse God and die. (Now here she is, I can imagine, sick and tired of going through the pain with her husband. So not only do she want her husband to give up on God, but she is ready to give up on God also to say such a thing. Listen, I don't care what pain and suffering you may face in your church or in your marriage or in your family, you do not turn your back on God. You do not give up on God. A lot of prayer and guidance from God can see you through the trying times. Remember God will direct our path as long as we put our trust in Him and acknowledge Him in all that we do.) Job replied, "Woman you're talking like a fool right now."

I am absolutely sure that I told my husband the same exact thing when he began to say some crazy things concerning God. I was literally afraid for him because I feared God. Not only was he not a God fearing man but he said some frightening things against God. Job never once said anything against God when hard times hit him. Job said, if we can accept blessings, we can accept troubles also. In other words, he is saying that troubles will not stop me from serving God.

What about you, when troubles or obstacles come your way, will you turn your back on God? Will you continue to serve Him and love Him no matter what the situation? We got to stop being like little wimps or crybabies when troubles or obstacles come our way. Life does get hard sometimes, but only the strong in Christ shall survive. I did a lot of crying through some of my trials. For instance, I cried a lot dealing with one of my children that is a diabetic. I have been in and out of the hospitals with him for years. I watched him suffer and suffer. This hurt me to the point that I began to suffer. I even questioned God about this situation. I thought enough is enough. Be careful not to lose your strength while going through. You may not even realize that your strength is gone. Satan will tempt you to turn away from God. That is his purpose. That is his goal. That is his intention.

Intentions

Do you know intentions alone can leave you in a terrible mess? Yes baby doll, intentions can leave you, your family, your friendships or anybody else in a terrible mess. Let's give three examples on how some folks word don't mean a thing. These situations may occur only because you put your trust in man and not God. The bible states that God shall supply all your needs. Man can never supply all your needs because a man is limited with his supplies. Man supplies will run out eventually but God supplies never runs out. So are you looking for God to supply your needs or are you constantly looking for man who is limited? Here are three examples of trusting in a person word alone.

(Example 1)

What if someone promised to help you with your electric bill and decided at the last minute to say, "I couldn't do it, but I had good intentions." What if they forgot or act like they forgot? Intentions just left you in a terrible mess. Why? It's because now your lights are out only because you believed and trusted their word. You depended on them and that hurts. Try to be a man or woman of your word. Don't speak too soon before you realize if in fact you can do it or not. Now we all know that there are some cases when other situations come up and you can't do it after you gave them your word. You meant well. It happens. This should be a lesson taught. Avoid putting all your trust in man who is limited but always depend whole heartily on God. God will see you through any situation. I remember getting my gas turned off. Guess what? God supplied me with hot water anyway. Now somebody ought to praise God for that! Thank you Jesus! My God is All Powerful and Almighty!

(Example 2)

What if you and Bill had decided to get married and both of you seemed to be very excited about it. You were wearing the ring that he bought you. All of the invitations were sent out. Bill all of a sudden decides to marry Sally instead and he broke off the engagement with you. Maybe he just liked the way Sally walked. You found out and confronted him even though God gave you a sign not to marry him right now. He is still under construction so wait. God needs to build more character in him. Bill said, "I had every intention on marrying you, and I'm serious, but things changed." Right there you should have said to yourself, thank God. You already saw the signs. Intentions left you in a terrible mess. Why? The reason is that God gave you signs not to go through with this marriage, yet you wanted to anyway to save yourself from embarrassment. You are so embarrassed, ashamed and heart broken. You now think that you are in a bad situation because you believed and trusted in his word. You depended on him not once seeking God about it. That hurts because you didn't acknowledge God from the start. The enemy put you in sleep mode and now you feel the need to cry. Go ahead and cry. After you have finished crying then don't stay there, get on with your life. Wipe your weeping eyes and put your hands on your hips don't let your backbone slip. It will be all right in the morning. Just keep your trust in God. He is willing and able to place you in a position to receive Mr. Right since your Mr. Right went wrong. You need to wait on God first because His timing is better than ours. When you realize and believe that your time is coming, then you can laugh and dance about it. Come on wipe your weeping eyes and put your hands on your hip don't let your backbone slip. Shake it to the east, shake it to the west, and shake it to the one that I (you) love the best. I love Almighty God the best! How about you who do you love the best? I pray that it is Our Father in Heaven. Hallelujah! Thank you Jesus for keeping me from making a big mistake. Thank you God for interrupting my plans.

(Example 3)

What if you had a young musician that just started playing for your local church. He seems to be very humble and likeable. Well one Sunday morning, he decided not to show up for church service when the choir, Pastor, and congregation awaits him. There was a no call and no show. The young musician says later, "I had every intention to be there, but I had promised another church that I would be there also. Now how can you be in two places at one time? Intentions left you in a terrible mess because now people are wondering if he is trustworthy or not. The choir was embarrassed, ashamed and hurt because the choir had to sing something totally different from what was rehearsed. And get this, the musician never decided to mention that he wasn't going to be there on Sunday morning. He had every chance to mention it during your Thursday night rehearsal. It hurts. All because you trusted and depended on him. Communication is so important. This could be a set up by the enemy to cause someone to get discouraged and give up. Communication is vital, but trust in the Lord with all your heart and lean not to your own understanding. This could also be a set up by God for the choir, the Pastor and the congregation to be stretched. So next time something like that occurs, then maybe you will say, "We don't need no music, just clap your hands." We also know that we can always purchase tracks from the Christian Bookstore all day long. So instead of complaining, be creative and put your trust in God.

Listen, the enemy is going to do everything possible to make you give up on God. He wants to make you turn away from God. That is the enemy intention. It is not a mistake. The enemy intends for you to turn your back on God. He will use anyone or certain situations to make it work. Look at (Example 2). Maybe God ordained this marriage and the enemy didn't like it. So the enemy places an enticing obstacle in the way, another woman. Maybe the other woman was extremely nice and pretty to him. Too pretty for him to resist, but yet she was a counterfeit. Listen ladies, If you choose to marry someone that is not spiritually mature enough to meet your needs, then he may find another little girlie that is too hard to resist.

If he is a baby Christian then he may not have the ability or strength to resist another woman yet. The reason is because that could have been one of his strongest weaknesses and the enemy will play on that. You better check it out before you sign on the dotted line. Now in this example, we will say he chose to get with the counterfeit. Maybe it was what she had to offer physically and not spiritually. Maybe she seemed to be well established with her own business, her own home, real estate properties, living in a big beautiful house and plenty of money to go along with it. That could have caught his attention. Maybe he hadn't realized that the woman he left had more to offer spiritually. All the material things could have come at a later time. Matthew 6: 33 reads, "But seek ye first the Kingdom of God, and his righteousness; and all these things shall be added unto you." Maybe he was just too impatient and couldn't wait. Well he didn't want to wait. He may have asked himself, "Why should I have to wait when I could have it all right now?" He could have actually had a spiritual lifestyle but made a bad choice. There would be more power in a marriage that God joined together and ordained. It would be better than any marriage that comes together when they are not equally yoked up together spiritually. The enemy knows that, so he will try to block an ordained marriage. Don't get weary, don't faint but keep walking and just wait on God because he shall renew your strength.

> *But they that wait upon the Lord shall*
> *renew their strength, they shall mount*
> *up with wings as eagles; they shall run*
> *and not be weary; and they shall walk,*
> *and not faint. Isaiah 40: 31*

A marriage could lead you to your destiny, or a marriage could lead you to destruction. Please do not try to force anyone to be with you. Do not, I repeat! Do not confront the other woman who you think is a threat and say to her, "God said that he is MY husband." Do not talk about the other woman because of your insecurities. You cannot force a man to love you. Throwing tantrums will not help the situation either. This is out of order. God doesn't need your help. God is God all by Himself. If God chose that man to be your husband and he gets out of the will, then start praying that he doesn't continue to give into the enemy tricks. If he does give into the enemy and get out of the will, then God can choose another husband. He can choose one that is even better for you. There may be a new memo out straight from heaven.

Don't get discouraged. Hang on in there. It can happen for you, but be watchful. Continue to pray and take your time. Even though God may choose someone for you, you have to make the final decision. I pray that you seek God and choose wisely. Proverbs 3:6 reads, "Acknowledge God in all thy ways and He shall direct your paths." We all need guidance from God. We all need some sense of direction. That's why we need to acknowledge Him in everything we do.

Chapter 17
GROWING UP

As a little girl, life was pretty easy for me. I had both parents in the home. It's sad to say that you don't find both parents in the home more so today. Maybe that could be part of the reason that our families are falling apart. My family consisted of six children including myself. I watched as my earthly father worked each and everyday. A hardworking man with strict rules. He was the disciplinary. Either you abide by the rules or get punished. That was how it was. He would say, "Either you do what I say as I say when I say or you will get punished!" We would suffer the wrath of our father that enforced rules if we didn't. If you thought you were too grown or high minded to abide by the rules then you can get out. Now we did joke around and laugh a lot but he and only he was the head ruler and man of the household. He was the head of the household but God was his head.

Your Pastor is the head of your church home and God should be his head. If you think you are too grown or high minded to abide by the rules of the church, then you don't have to stay because your mother stayed. You don't have to stay because Auntie Shirley stayed. You don't have to stay because Grandma stayed. You can get to stepping so that maybe you will begin to step into some light. You cannot take your Pastors place. Even if you do have a lot of knowledge of the word you cannot take his or her place. Even if you think you heard from God you cannot take your Pastors place and override their vision. That is out of order. If this is you then you need to be disciplined. Maybe you are more knowledgeable of the word. It doesn't matter how much of Gods' word you know, you cannot run the house. The same thing applies in the workplace. You cannot take your boss's place. He should be respected of his position. If you don't like the way your boss is running things then get out. No one is making you stay. Now I am not suggesting you let them run over you. If you think you have out grown a certain position then you can leave. That reminds me of the story of Lucifer (Satan). He had fallen out of heaven because he became high minded and prideful. He thought he could be equal to The Most High. He just thought he was too grown.

> *Isaiah 14: 12-14*
> *How art thou fallen from heaven, O Lucifer*
> *son of the morning! How art thou cut down*
> *to the ground, which didst weaken the*
> *nations! (Lucifer is a name applied to as*
> *Satan). (verse 12)*
>
> *For thou hast said in thine heart, I will*
> *ascend into heaven, I will exalt my throne*
> *above the stars of God: I will sit also upon*
> *the mount of the congregation, in the sides*
> *of the north: (verse 13)*
>
> *I will ascend above the heights of the clouds,*
> *I will be like the most High. (verse 14)*

Pride got in the way of Lucifer. He used to have sight since he was the son of the morning. He used to have correct vision since there was light. The son of the morning has fallen from the sky! Lucifer brought down nations and now to this day he is brought down. To this very day, the enemy is still trying to bring down nations. The enemy (Lucifer or Satan) is now deep in the world of the dead. He decided, "I don't have to deal with this anymore." He's saying, "I am just as good as God Almighty." Wrong attitude. He's saying, "I am mighty myself because I am the star." It sounds like he got drunk off himself and went to sleep. He's saying, "Why should I have to listen to God. I could be just as high as God can and maybe even higher." He's saying, "I will exalt my own throne." He's saying, "I will exalt myself." You young ministers out there, be very careful of this. Self-exaltation got in the way which caused him to fall from heaven. Heaven used to be his home until he changed. Lucifer caused himself to be put into sleep mode due to his greediness. This is the state some of us get in while under the leadership in our own home church, in the workplace and even in a marriage. The enemy had to get him some gone (slang for flee or depart) because our Father in heaven don't play that.

Now there is a flip side to all this. There are some Pastors today that are exalting themselves. They want to take the place of God. They come up with their own plans that are not Gods plans. This is a dangerous state to be in. Some people in leadership act just like Pharaoh. They lift themselves up. They work on pleasing themselves and man rather than God. They think that they are just as good at making their own plans rather than doing it Gods way. They want to be the star. They are stealing Gods glory. What happens is, when God send them a Moses to tell them, "God said, let my people go, so they may serve and worship me," then they tend to get very angry. What God is saying is, if my people are not allowed to serve and worship me, then let them go. Let them out of bondage. Some leaders will look at the Moses that God sent to get a message to them as if to say, "Who are you?" "Who do you think you are?" They may say, "You are beneath me because

I am running this and you have to go along with my plan," never once opening their ears and eyes to Gods plan. From their actions it seems like some of the leaders are thinking, "Why should I have to listen to God when I am your God." They may even show signs that they want all the attention rather than giving God the glory.

Many leaders of today have become very prideful. They think no one can teach them anything, especially a woman. Honey, we can learn from a baby. Some have gotten so high minded and puffed up that they probably are thinking, "I built this church and I got all the members." "This is my congregation." "I have the largest church in the district." What happens is that they become very prideful and they make it their ambition to be a god to the congregation. They will begin to self exalt themselves. Some have actually turned the pulpit into a pit of thieves. It has become a pit from hell. If you are not careful then this will cause you to fall into a pit. The reason is because you chose to walk in disobedience by walking in darkness. Lucifer fell from being so wicked and prideful. Believe me you can show this attitude without even saying a word.

You forgot that God said, If I be lifted up, I would draw all men unto me. Those of you who are wondering about your membership, God said, He would draw the people if you lift Him up! God will draw your wife closer to you if you lift Him up. If you continue to lift yourself up and become so prideful, then this can cause a separation or even cause one to scatter. Jeremiah 23:1 states, "Woe unto the pastors (or leaders) that destroy and scatter the sheep of my pasture! Said the Lord." This is a warning because woe indicates that somebody is going to regret what he or she has done and be punished in some way. Woe also means grief or distress resulting from a serious affliction or misfortune. The dictionary states that the speaker will begin to feel unhappy or unfortunate. Be careful leaders! Do not let denomination or tradition get in the way of you following God! Do not walk around with an UN-teachable spirit because you do not know it all. Stay humble and walk in love. Even though you are the ruler or the leader like Pharaoh was then you can bring a curse on the house if you are not careful. Do not let tradition get in the way of you following God all because you were taught or raised that way. Please don't let it get in the way of you being obedient to God, our Father. It can mess you up! Some of us do not know how to walk in love. Please let us learn how to walk in love.

> *I Corinthians 13:1-8, 13*
> *Though I speak with the tongues of men*
> *and of angels, and have not charity (love),*
> *I am become as sounding brass, or a*
> *tinkling cymbal. (verse 1)*

In other words, It doesn't matter how many languages you speak or how articulate you are. If you do not have brotherly or sisterly love for one another, then you will be nothing more than a noisy gong or clanging cymbal. It will be like you are talking loud and saying nothing. The reason is because your words hold no weight due to the lack of brotherly or sisterly love. So shhhhhhh, be quiet. We don't want to hear you right now until you get this love walk in order. Could you please shut that bad attitude up? This is required for any relationship that we are in, whether it is with a husband, wife, children, parents, etc. The relationship could be with a pastor and congregation. It could be the workplace or even business partners. Is there any love in the house? If not, then you can find where the conflict lies. I know that I don't want to be up close and personal with anyone that creates a hostile environment for me. What about you, do you like conflict?

> *And though I have the gift of prophecy,*
> *and understand all mysteries, and all*
> *knowledge, and though I have all faith,*
> *so that I could remove mountains, and*
> *have not charity (love), I am nothing.*
> *I Corinthians 13: 2*

What if you could prophesy and understand all secrets and all knowledge? What if you have spiritual discernment? What if you have faith that could move mountains. You will be nothing unless you love others. It does not matter how great your faith is, you still must have love.

> *And though I bestow all my goods to feed*
> *the poor, and though I give my body to be*
> *burned, and have not charity (love), it*
> *profiteth me nothing. I Corinthians 13: 3*

What if you made a sacrifice to feed the poor? That's good. What if you sacrificed and gave an offering when you really didn't have it to give? That's good. You will gain nothing from doing all that unless you love others. Your harvest will not come if you do not love others.

> *Charity (love) suffereth long, and is kind;*
> *charity (love) envieth not, charity (love)*
> *vaunteth not itself, is not puffed up.*
> *I Corinthians 13: 4*

Love is kind and patient. Love is never jealous or envious. Love is never boastful or proud. How many of you have been married to someone that was jealous and envious of you? How many of you were jealous of your spouse? It is not an easy thing to swallow is it? Love will never get jealous of anyone. Love will never be envious of what you do or what you have. Love is never prideful.

> *Doth not behave itself unseemly, seeketh*
> *not her own, is not easily provoked,*
> *thinketh no evil; I Corinthians 13: 5*

Love is not rude and will not disrespect you. If someone disrespects you and tell you that they love you then they are lying through their teeth. Love is not selfish. Do you know anybody that is selfish and stingy? If so then that is not love. I remember asking somebody that I was in relationship with for fifty cents. Do you know he told me no! All because he wanted me to suffer. That is not love. Love is not quick tempered or easily provoked.

> *Rejoiceth not in iniquity, but rejoiceth in*
> *the truth; I Corinthians 13: 6*

Love rejoices in the truth. Love rejoices when you are obedient and walking upright before God. Love does not rejoice in evil and wrongdoings. How many people do you know get happy when they see somebody doing wrong? They are definitely out there. I see some men that rejoice in seeing another man play on the ladies. I hope you are not one of them. There is nothing cute about being unfaithful and rejoicing about it.

> *Beareth all things, believeth all things,*
> *hopeth all things endureth all things.*
> *I Corinthians 13: 7*

Love is always supportive. Is your husband or wife always supportive of you when you choose to live a godly lifestyle? I didn't always have that with my spouse and that made it hard for me sometimes. Love is always loyal. Is your husband or wife always loyal or truthful to you? Love is always hopeful and trusting. Is your spouse always truthful and trusting with you? They should be. Is your family always supportive? Love is supportive. In a healthy marriage you ought to be able to support one another. Now we know you can't support a liar and a cheat.

> *Charity (love) never faileth; but whether*
> *there be prophecies, they shall fail;*
> *whether there be tongues, they shall cease;*
> *whether there be knowledge, it shall vanish*
> *away. I Corinthians 13: 8*

Prophecies shall fail and unknown tongues shall fail but one thing for sure, LOVE never fails. You may not have all knowledge but one thing for sure LOVE never fails. You cannot go wrong with love because it will not let you down. If you really love someone you will not let him or her down by lying and cheating on them. You will not let them down by abusing them. You will never disrespect them.

> *And now abideth faith, hope, charity (love),*
> *these three, but the greatest of these is*
> *charity (love). I Corinthians 13: 13*

This is saying even though you have faith that is great. Even though you have spiritual hope that is great. The fact that you have loved that is great. All three are important but love is preeminent. Love stands out because it is superior of the three. The greatest of all three is love. You must love with a pure heart.

Sometimes we think that it is all about us. We need to grow up and realize that it is not all about us. It is not all about you.

You are not the star. It is not all about me. I am not the star. The only star is my Lord and Savior Jesus Christ. We must walk in the will of God with love. You don't walk in His will with an attitude. God is not making you serve Him. It was your choice so be happy about it. It is very important to walk in love. Remember love never fails. Search yourself. Are you walking in Gods will or not? Are you walking in love or not? If not, then maybe you are still young spiritually. Maybe you are just a babe in Christ. Maybe you are an immature Christian, if in fact you are a Christian at all. Now you can fool some of the people some of the time, but you cannot fool God none of the time. Hello somebody! Perhaps you don't know if you are walking in the will of God or not. If you are not walking in love then you are not walking in His will completely. Could it be that you don't realize that you are walking at all because you are sleepwalking? If this is you then this is a wake up call. Its time to wake up and grow up!

> *And that, knowing the time, that now it is high time to awake out of sleep: For now is our salvation nearer than when we believed. Romans 13:11*

Now we know what kind of times we are living in, so we should be mindful to live properly. It's time to wake up! We know that the day that Christ returns is soon to come. Night is almost over, and day will soon appear. We must stop behaving as people do in the dark and be ready to live in the light. So behave properly, as people do in the day. Let the Lord, Jesus Christ be as near to you as the clothes you have on you back. Then you won't try to satisfy your selfish desires. We must be trained properly how to live and love. If we are not trained properly, then the weight will come. And nobody likes to be overweight.

Physical Training versus Spiritual Training

In training, we know that we all have to start somewhere. We must start at the beginning and work our way up to become physically or spiritually fit. In training you must take your time, stay focused and gradually build yourself up to the next level humbly. We must all continue to be in training until the end of time. There is no one that has attained it all. No not one. But you must have a teachable spirit.

When I first started my physical training class, it was a struggle just to go to the gym or even work out at home. There were so many other things that I could be doing. I had to make time. I had to discipline myself. I had to have determination. I needed to be motivated. When I finally got there, aerobics was on. It made me feel good about myself. I realized that the weight didn't come off in one day. I had to continue to work at it to actually see some results. But when the results came, I was very happy about what I had accomplished. Even though you see results, you should continue to stay in training or the weight will come back soon.

Let me give you an example of when I was a young little girl that tried to ride a bicycle for the first time. The very first time I had training wheels on so that I could have balance. Now we must be trained so that we could be educated and prepared to go to the next level. After I learned how to ride with the training wheels I gained confidence in riding. Now I was ready to go to the next level. So they then took the training wheels off. It seemed a little shaky at first because it was new to me. But soon I became confident in riding without the training wheels. As I grew older, I kept going to the next level. Next I could go from a 3 speed, to a 5 speed, or to a 10 speed. Now this is not to say that you will never get tired because in most cases you will, but don't give up.

When I first started my spiritual walk, it was a struggle just to pick my bible up and read it on my own. It was also a struggle to watch the church channels. Now I don't go to bed without it. I had to discipline myself. I had to have determination. I had to be motivated. When I finally got into the habit of reading my holy bible and studying it, then it was on like popcorn. It was popping baby. Sometimes the enemy would try to put me to sleep. There were times that the enemy did put me to sleep, but I had determination. Even if I had to read the same passage of scriptures over five times until I got it. I had to continue to read it, speak it, and walk it. I couldn't let the enemy get the best of me. If he knocked me down, then I would get back up fighting. I would begin to see results. Not only would I see the results, but others could also see the results in my life. I would let my light shine. You must remember that you should have a balanced life. Even though you may see results, you must continue to stay in training. If you don't then the weights of this world may come so heavy on you, that you may not be spiritually strengthened enough to handle it. For instance, when you are a babe in Christ, as you grow older and you have been in training, then you know that you must wear the whole armor of God. The reason is so that you may be able to stand against the wiles (tricks) of the devil.

As you grow older in Christ, I'm sure you will learn to cast down imaginations when the enemy interjects thoughts in your mind. As you grow older, you will continue to go from one level to another. Remember new levels new devils.

God will continue to educate and prepare you as long as you continue to stay in training. Remember that anything that is connected to God is always growing. So if you are growing then you are always changing. Please understand change can do you some good.

House Rules

> *Train up a child in the way he should*
> *go: and when he is old, he will not*
> *depart from it. Proverbs 22:6*

Rules are made to protect you. Parents teach your children right from wrong while they are young. So when they are grown they should do right even if they get off track sometimes. Even though it takes some of us longer than others to get back on the right track. I say that because we get stubborn or rebellious sometimes. I thank God for the prayers that went up for me because at one point in my life, I turned my back on God out of ignorance. Even though I was brought up in the church all my life, I strayed away because I wanted to do what I wanted to do. But I found my way back into a place with God that I would never leave. I am nothing without Him. I love God with all my heart. So when you see your children stray away from God, even though you trained them properly, keep praying for them and don't give up. They will come back to a place where they first received Him. They just have some growing up to do. We must stay hopeful and pray that it won't be too late because maturity can take years.

When I was a child, there was discipline in our home. We were not allowed to even frown in our father's presence unless we were sick. That's when mother steps in. By the way, our mother's name for us was Mother. While growing up we were teased about calling our mother, Mother. They would ask us, "Do you call your father, Father?" No we did not. My mother was the type of woman that showed us love at all times even when we thought our father was mean to us. She never punished us but granted us an abundance of love.

My mother is a meek and humble woman. Soft spoken mostly. You would hardly ever hear her raise her voice at us. All she had to say was, "I'm going to tell your father." Oh but you know what, it worked. That statement really worked. It was something about that statement that changed our whole attitude. You see I loved my earthly father, but I feared him and his commandments (rules). So I would straighten up and act right. We should also fear our heavenly father. We should act right and sin not.

> *The fear of the Lord is the beginning of*
> *knowledge; but fools despise wisdom*
> *and instruction. Proverbs 1:7*

> *For the wages of sin is death; but the gift*
> *of God is eternal life through Jesus Christ*
> *our Lord. Romans 6:23*

When you begin to fear and respect the Lord, then this is the beginning of knowledge. A fool is somebody who lacks good sense or judgement. A fool is unintelligent or a thoughtless person. A fool could care less about you trying to give them godly wisdom or godly advice. A fool behaves irresponsibly. A fool fools around with other fools. A fool wastes time by doing silly or unimportant things. A fool has casual and unprotected sex like it is nothing. They don't even realize or think that they could become HIV positive. You cannot just look at people and tell if they are HIV positive or not. People that have contracted this disease or any other disease are having casual and unprotected sex more and more today without telling the other partner.

Listen, if you continue to work sin and work sin overtime, then your salary or payment in return will be death. I say that because the wages of sin is death. You need to know that death could mean spiritually or physically. Parents you should have house rules. We as parents should obey them first before we can expect our children to do so. We are to be examples for our children. If you are doing any and everything under the sun, then what do you expect your children to do? They are watching you. So Pastors, you are to be examples for the children in the house of God. Likewise husbands, you are to be examples for your wife and children. They are looking at an image, and you should love your wife as Christ loves the church. Meaning that you are willing to die for her. They ought to be able to see that godly image on a regular basis and not when you are just around church folk. Don't put on a front. Don't wear a mask. We were really taught discipline in our home. We were taught to respect people and especially our elders. That is still in me today.

Ephesians 6:2-3
Honor thy father and mother; which is
the first commandment with promise;
(verse 2)

That it may be well with thee, and thou
mayest live long on the earth. (verse 3)

If you want to live a long and happy life, then honor your parents. Now honor means to respect highly. Even though you should respect and honor your parents highly, please be careful not to follow some of their bad habits. Parents how can you train your children if you don't even spend time with them? If you gave birth to them then it is your job to train them. How can a child be trained if a parent is absent in their lives? And yet you try to justify why you are not there. Now there are some situations that couldn't be helped but on the other hand, there are those that have no excuse! The devil is a liar! You do not punish your children because you made some bad choices. God is watching you. If you are the Christian that you say you are then that should bother you. It should bother you to a point that you would want to do something about it.

One rule that stuck with me in our home was never to tell a lie. There are a lot of homes missing that one rule. Oh you may say technically no one wants to be lied to, but people we accept it anyway. We sometimes even give excuses for telling a lie and even living a lie. It is wrong, and there is no excuse for it. Trust me, you will pay for it.

There was something about lying that really affected and bothered my earthly father in a mighty way. It really hurt him. So now I'm wondering and meditating on this word called lie. What is a lie? A lie is defined as 1) an assertion of something known or believed by the speaker to be true with intent to deceive, 2) an untrue or inaccurate statement that may or may not be believed true by the speaker, 3) something that misleads or deceives. I'm wondering now would this affect our heavenly father? If so, then how would it affect Him? I found out that the word lie is such a small word, but can cause great destruction. Lets look at the character of Satan (the enemy) and his attributes. First he is the father of lies and secondly he is a deceiver.

*Ye are of your father the devil, and the
lusts of your father ye will do. He was
a murderer from the beginning, and
abode not in the truth, because there is
no truth in him. When he speaketh a
lie, he speaketh of his own: for he is a
liar, and the father of it. John 8:44*

Who is your father? I know that some people don't know
whom their father is so let's find out. First, let us make up
in our mind that we will not become a liar or even live a lie
like the enemy who is the father of lies. God did not say in
His word that it's all right to lie if it means saving someone's
feelings. God's word does not say that it is all right to lie with
intent to deceive or mislead someone. People it is not good
to lie just to gain brownie points. The bible says if you are a
liar, your father or daddy is the devil (the enemy). Now do
you know who your father is?

We all know that God cannot lie. So if you continue to lie
after knowing better, then maybe you like doing exactly what
your daddy, the devil wants you to do. The reason is because
you lust after the same things your father the devil lust after.
Did you know that lies could kill? Maybe you killed someone
with your lies. I hope not. There is nothing truthful about
the enemy. He has been a murderer from the beginning. The
bible dictionary states that to lie means to intentionally tell an
untruth. This is the nature of the enemy. You are classified as a
liar when you deny that Jesus is Christ. You are classified as a
liar when you are not keeping Gods commandments. You are
classified as a liar when you hate your brother or sister. You
are classified as a liar when you are out of the will of God.

I John 4:20-21
If a man say, I love God, and hateth his
brother, (hate your mother, father, sister,
children, etc.) he is a liar: for he that
loveth not his brother whom he hath
seen, how can he love God whom he
hath not seen? (verse 20)

And this commandment have we from
him, That he who loveth God love his
brother also. (verse 21)

Secondly, another characteristic of the enemy is that he is a deceiver. A deceiver is one who misleads others. In the third chapter of the book of Genesis, Satan lied and deceived Eve in the Garden of Eden. The enemy has been lying and deceiving us since the beginning of time. The devil was cast out of heaven. So if you brought the devil into your home and married him, then maybe you need to cast him out. Cast him and his partners out! And you were wondering why you and your children are being attacked. Those are your children, so don't let the devil separate you from them. If the man just wants you and not your children, then you got the wrong one baby! Uh-huh! If he says he loves you but not your children, then the devil is a liar!

The enemy is trying to deceive you, especially if you go along with leaving your children behind. Oh honey, some of you get so caught up in wanting to have a man so bad, that you actually neglect your own children. Some of you get caught up in wanting to live the life of the rich and famous that you tend to neglect your children. Some of you will buy nice clothes to look good for a man and let your children look shabby or even let them go without. In some cases, some of you will actually take food from your baby's mouth in order to give it to your man. The devil is a liar! You need to wake up because you are sleeping hard if this is you. You are probably even snoring very loud. Wake up! Stop sleeping with the enemy who has knocked you unconscious!

Another example is you leaving your children with your parents while you drift away into the sunset. Maybe the man put you in a beautiful home without your children. Why can't your children enjoy that beautiful home with you? Wake up and see that the enemy is running circles around your head. You must be confused, and I know the devil is the author of confusion. Don't let the devil confuse you anymore. Maybe you need to smack yourself because your babies really need you. Stop being deceived and tricked. What you need to do is cast that sneaky slimy snake out of your life along with his partners. Cast them out! They must go today!

> *And the great dragon was cast out, that*
> *old serpent, called the Devil, and Satan,*
> *which deceiveth the whole world: he was*
> *cast out into the earth, and his angels*
> *were cast out with him.*
> *Revelation 12:9*

Satan strives to keep you bound so that you cannot have the finer things in life. Sometimes all the talking, teaching and preaching in the world couldn't help you because your heart is not open to receive. We can talk to you all night, all week, all month and all year and it still won't register because you are so clogged up and polluted with so much mess. You must be wearing those clogs we spoke about in the previous chapters. Take those shoes off would you please? Why? The reason is because your feet must be stinking by the way that you are walking. Some way or some how your feet must have gotten a little dusty by the way you are walking. People, in the name of the Father, the Son and the Holy Ghost, wake up and stop sleeping with the enemy destroying and ruining your life! The enemy will make you stink really badly! Get rid of the terrible odor! It stinks!

The enemy will set you up. The enemy can influence someone to say that they love you and yet hate you at the same time. It is a trap by the mean, the bad, the ugly and stinking, Satan! You have been set up and you fell for it. Get out before it is too late! Make up in your mind that enough is enough! It is high time, and I will say it again, it is high time to wake up out of sleep! People you have been sleeping too long with the enemy who is trying to destroy your life.

You have now developed cravings for that junk Satan (the enemy) likes. I call it junk food. Junk food can bring you a lot of weight. You have been feeding off this junk food that the world provides for you and the one who is feeding it to you don't like you anyway. People, the enemy does not like you! He is just using you to do his will and you fell in the trap. Some of you fell so deep in the trap that it brought layers of thickness to your head. Not only is the enemy using you, but he got you using other people also. I definitely wouldn't want to be in your shoes of helping the enemy develop his army. You need to get off the losing team and get on the winning team. If you stay in this state of mind or situation, you will lose in the end. The time is now to make a change. You must change your way of thinking. Your mind needs to be renewed. Ask yourself, "Why am I craving this junk?" "Why am I allowing people to issue me junk?" I'll tell you why. It is because you have allowed the enemy to slip into the cracks somewhere and somehow.

And be not conformed to this world: but be ye transformed by the renewing of your mind, that ye may prove what is that good, and acceptable and perfect, will of God. Romans 12:2

You need to find out what is acceptable to God and do that. What is Gods will for you? Everything you do is not acceptable to God. Some of your minds need to be transformed and renewed. Some of you need a complete change because your thinking could be stinking right now. Some of you take the word lie ever so lightly. That small word not only causes destruction to other people which you will be responsible for, but it also causes destruction to you. I hope you are not wearing the pants that will be on fire for becoming a liar. You know the saying, "Liar, liar pants on fire!" There is a real lake of fire waiting on all liars. You need to choose this day that you will serve our Lord and Savior, Jesus Christ.

Tomorrow is not promised to you. If the enemy is your partner, then he will try in every way to kill you. The enemy comes to kill, steal and destroy. He will steal your virginity, he will steal your husband or your wife. The enemy will steal your children, your entire family and your life if you allow it. The enemy will have some of you convincing people to get on drugs to increase your finances. The enemy will convince you that drugs and alcohol can solve all your problems or at least soothe the pain. The devil is a liar!

If you are a partaker of convincing people to live unrighteous, then that will be on your hands and you don't want that. You will be held responsible when the real judge comes. God is going to judge you and you alone. You cannot stand with anyone else. Trust me this is real. Your father can't stand with you. Your mother can't stand with you. Your husband or wife cannot stand with you. Your brother, sister or children will not be able to stand with you. On the day of judgement you must and will stand-alone. I pray that God open your eyes and ears to understand enough to make a complete change.

Turn that negative energy around from convincing people to live unrighteous to encouraging them to live righteous. Tell them that Jesus is the reason you have your life, health and strength. Let them know that Jesus is a way maker. Some people think that you have to sleep around with somebody to get your bills paid. If you just trust God, He will make a way out of no way. Jesus can and shall supply all your needs. All you have to do is put your trust in Him and He can see you through any situation.

The enemy can have your mind destroyed by thinking that you can deceive or lie to anybody and get away with it. Oh but no! God is omniscient which means having infinite awareness, understanding, and insight. God possesses a complete knowledge of the universe. So maybe you can fool man but you can't fool God. This is a trap by your so-called friend Satan. Another oops upside the head okay? Satan and his angels are probably standing on the sidelines singing oops upside your head, I said oops upside your head. Say what? I can picture them all laughing at you. They're all gonna laugh at you! You might as well put yourself inside the lollipop (sucker), because that's what he's calling us when we don't know any better. He's making a nuisance out of us! Meaning we become harmful, annoying, unpleasant, obnoxious and even a pest. We must wake up and admit that we need help.

People you must open your mouth and admit that you need help. After you admit that you need help, then come to reality and realize that you are not as strong as you think you are.

You do not possess the power to help yourself totally. Let me say that again. You do not possess the power to help yourself totally. It goes beyond having all the money in the world. It goes beyond having and possessing all the name brand shoes or clothes. It goes beyond having all the degrees you can acquire. It goes beyond being the most popular preacher. It goes beyond being the best football player, basketball player, golf player or a pimp player. We have to admit that we need help.

I cried out to God one day because I knew that I needed help. Now I have in my possession the best friend I could ever have in the whole world. His name is Jesus! Thank you Lord for Jesus! Thank you for saving me Lord. Thank you for filling me with your Holy Spirit. People we must be born again and filled with his precious Holy Spirit. We must be rooted and grounded in Gods word so that when the enemy began to attack us, we will know how to attack him back with scripture.

If we want help, we need to keep our joy of praise no matter what the circumstance. Pray without ceasing. When some of your earthly friends began to act a little funny, then you can call on Jesus. He will never leave you nor forsake you. Wouldn't it be nice to be married to someone who has the mind of Christ. One who will never leave you nor forsake you? One who would stay with you through thick and thin until God calls them home? One who would be loyal and true to you because of their covenant with God? You don't have to worry about Jesus acting funny because He is a true friend. When people misunderstand you, you can call on Jesus. When people mistreat you, you can call on Jesus. When someone lies on you or lies to you, then you can call on Jesus. Jesus will help see you through any given situation. But remember to give

God the entire honor, glory and the praise. Please don't ever forget that God is our Divine Helper. At one time or another we may just need some back up. We can say boldly that God is our Divine Helper. When we get needy sometimes, then know that help is on the way for Gods' children. So don't fear what man shall do to you. But be absolutely sure that your heart trusts God. You need to know that God can deliver you out of any situation.

> *So that we may boldly say, The Lord is*
> *my helper, and I will not fear what man*
> *shall do unto me. Hebrews 13:6*

> *Behold, the Lord God will help me; who*
> *is he that shall condemn me? Lo, they all*
> *shall wax old garment; the moth shall eat*
> *them up. Isaiah 50:9*

> *Fear thou not; for I am with thee: be not*
> *dismayed; For I am thy God: I will*
> *strengthen thee; yea, I will help thee; yea*
> *I will uphold thee with the right hand of*
> *my righteousness. Isaiah 41:10*

> *But I am poor and needy, yet the Lord*
> *thinketh upon me: thou art my help and*
> *my deliverer, make no tarrying, O my*
> *God. Psalms 40:17*

The Lord is my strength and my shield;
my heart trusted in him, and I am helped:
therefore my heart greatly rejoiceth; and
with my song will I praise him.
Psalms 28:7

All you have to do is keep your mind stayed on Jesus. Walk after the spirit and not the flesh because the flesh can get you in trouble. I was at work one day and a young lady asked me how do you walk in the spirit? I then led her to the book of Galatians, chapter five. Gods' spirit makes us loving, happy, peaceful, patient, kind, good, faithful, gentle and self-controlled. You must kill the flesh daily when it comes to your selfish feelings or desires. Don't be conceited or make others jealous by claiming to be better than they are. If your flesh begin to cause you to get out of order, then call on your divine helper, Jesus. If your flesh is controlling you then evidently you need some back up.

Chapter 18
RESPECT YOUR MARRIAGE

*Marriage is honorable in all, and the bed
undefiled: but whoremongers and adulterers
God will judge. Hebrew 13:4 (KJV)*

*Have respect for marriage. Always be faithful
to your partner, because God will punish
anyone who is immoral or unfaithful in
marriage. Hebrew 13:4 (CEV)*

What is marriage? First of all marriage is to be honored and respected. Even though God honors marriage, God does not honor all marriages. For example God does not honor male and male. God does not honor female and female. God does not honor you with a beast, an animal or a monster. There are even some male and female relationships that God does not honor.

God does not honor the marriage with a beast because the beast makes war with the saints. The beast is the instinctive irrational or aggressive part of somebody's personality. The beast is a brutal person. It is a cruel or aggressive person. They are extremely ruthless or cruel. They are unrelentingly harsh and severe. They are direct or insensitive in manner of speech. They are just brutally frank. This is typical for beasts. You are not to have sexual relations with the beast so that means don't marry one.

Leviticus 18: 23
Neither shalt thou lie with any beast to
defile thyself therewith: neither shall
any woman stand before a beast to lie
down thereto: it is confusion.

Anyone who has sex with a beast will become unclean. The people that are considered to be beasts made themselves and the land unclean. Do not do these sickening things to make the land filthy. Obey Gods laws. If you continue to lie with a beast anyway then there is a death penalty.

Leviticus 20: 15
And if a man lie with a beast, he shall
surely be put to death: and ye shall
slay the beast.

Leviticus 20: 16
And if a woman approach unto any
beast, and lie down thereto, thou shalt
kill the woman, and the beast: they
shall surely be put to death: their
blood shall be upon them.

So if any of you have sex with a beast then both you and the beast will be put to death if you are not careful. The scripture also states that you will try to slay the beast. That is why it is so important to choose wisely before entering into a relationship. Whatever you decide to do, please don't marry a beast! The beast will not honor and respect you!

Revelation 12: 9
And the great dragon was cast out,
that old serpent, called the Devil,
and Satan, which deceiveth the whole
world: he was cast out into earth, and
his angels were cast out with him.

The dragon lost the battle. The enemy and its angels were forced out of their places in heaven and were thrown down to earth. Yes, that old snake and his angels were thrown out of heaven. Now lets pull the covers off the animals because God does not honor the marriage with an animal. Animals are domesticated and wild. An animal is somebody who is vulgar or brutish. They belong to the realm of instincts and urges. That's why it is so important not to get into a relationship with an animal. Dragons or animals are vicious sea creatures. They are wild asses in high places.

Jeremiah 14: 6
And the wild asses did stand in the high
places, they snuffed up the wind like
dragons; their eyes did fail, because
there was no grass.

Maybe you thought the grass was greener on the other side but you came to realize that there was no grass at all. After you entered into a relationship like this all you saw was dirt and a lot of it. All the animal wants to do is stand in the high place of being your authority so you can be destroyed. Listen, wild asses go blind from starvation. So they stand on barren hilltops and sniff the air, hoping to smell green grass since Satan is the prince of the air. Stop being so green in the enemy's eyes. Wake up and get some understanding! Why? It is because Satan persecutes the woman. Did you know that?

Revelation 12: 13
And when the dragon saw that he was
cast unto the earth, he persecuted the
woman which brought forth the man
child.

Revelation 12: 17
And the dragon was wroth with the
woman, and went to make war with
the remnant of her seed, which keep
the commandments of God, and have
the testimony of Jesus Christ.

Are you hearing this my sisters? The enemy will attack you and your seed as long you keep the commandments of God. It is because you are producing fruit and he does not like that. He will attack you as long as your testimony is Jesus Christ because he is so angry with you for choosing to live godly. He is especially angry with you for bringing forth seed. Wow! This blew my mind! Especially after my son and I have been attacked so heavily. Please don't get in a relationship with an animal. It won't work. An animal will not honor or respect you!

God does not honor the marriage with a monster. Please, I beg of you, don't get in a relationship with a monster. God wouldn't want that. Why? The reason is because a monster is any ugly terrifying creature, animal or person. A monster is something fierce that kills people. The enemy comes to kill, steal and destroy you. A monster is an evil person. It is somebody whose inhumanity or vicious behavior terrifies and disgusts people. Just watching them operate will be so disgusting. It is somebody that is undesirably formed. They are animalistically carnal. They are so brutal that you can relate them to the beast. I don't want to be marked for life. I don't want to be marked for choosing with my flesh. I do not want the mark of the beast. The monster is cruel, ruthless and insensitive. They are crude and unintelligent. They lack sensitivity. They are shocking and morally unacceptable. It will leave a bad taste in your mouth. They are wicked and cruel. They are extremely unusual. They are greatly different from the norm. Whatever you decide to choose please don't choose a monster. It will be hazardous to your health because a monster will not honor or respect you! Don't let the enemy put you in sleep mode. Why would you choose someone like this to be your authority anyway?

My bible dictionary states that marriage is wedlock. It is the institution by which men and women are joined together and then they form a family. Now lets break the word wedlock down. Wed means to become married to somebody or two people joined together in marriage. Lock means to secure. To put in a safe and secure place. A woman always wants to feel a sense of security. We may ask the question, "After I marry you, am I locked in a safe place?" Inquiring minds want to know! Lock also means to prevent unauthorized use.

Since God is our authority, then He has the right to command. He has the right or power to enforce rules or give orders. He is the holder of all power. He is our source of reliable information on any subject. He knows the necessary ingredients that are needed in each individual to make the marriage work. Jesus is definitely one of the necessary ingredients needed for a happy and successful marriage. If you want Gods love then you need the spirit of God. God wants to be a part of your choosing. He has a quality that is and should be respected. He also has the ability to gain the respect of other people and to influence or control what they do. He has power that is legitimate because He is all-powerful. He will let you know what is unauthorized. He will let you know that you do not have permission to do that but you do have permission to do this. God should institute a marriage.

Genesis 2:18 states, "And the Lord God said, It is not good that the man should be alone, I *will make* him a help meet for him." "*Will make*" means that God is willing to appoint, organize, place, rule and set up that special person you should marry. Why do you say that? I'll tell you why. It is because God knows all the laws of love. Listen, you will have no power if you step out of the love of God. God is love. So if God is in control of your life, do you think that He wants you to marry a monster? No, I don't think so! So be very careful when you choose.

Genesis 2:24 states, "Therefore shall a man leave his father and his mother, and shall cleave unto his wife and they shall be one flesh." It is the husbands' duty to leave the office of clinging to mommy and daddy. He must stop holding on to mommy and daddy and become a responsible adult for his own marriage and family. Mom and Dad, it is alright to release your son to cleave to his wife. It does not mean that he loves you any less but the bible states that after marriage, his duty now is to cleave to his wife. Cleave means to cling closely, steadfastly and faithfully to your spouse. Cling means that you have to have a sticking quality. You must stick to it or stay very close to it and hold on tight.

That means that if you have a disagreement, and there will be some disagreements, then you don't automatically run home to mommy and daddy. You don't tell mommy and daddy all of your business. Steadfast means to be firm and unwavering in purpose, loyalty and resolve. You are to be stable and not easily moved. You must come to a firm decision that you are determined with purpose to follow the laws of love. Faithful is being consistently loyal. Consistently loyal! It is being consistently trustworthy, especially to a person, a promise and a duty. When the two of you made that covenant, then it was as to God and not man. Let me say it again, it was as to God and not man. So when you break the agreement or covenant with God's chosen spouse, then you have broken the agreement with God.

What does it mean to be faithful? Faithful is not being promiscuous. It is not having sexual relations with somebody other than your spouse. Being faithful should be conscientious between both individuals. It is displaying or resulting from a sense of responsibility or devotion to duty. It is the husband and the wife duty to be faithful to one another because of the covenant you made unto God. Faithful is to be correct, accurate and true. Faithful is somebody that is reliable. Can you rely on one another? It is someone you can depend on and can be trusted. Can you depend on and trust one another? A marriage should be honored. There should be a permanent bond. There should be an intimate bond. A marriage is blessed of God for having children. A marriage should be dissolved by death (spiritual or physical). Marriage is a means of sexual love. Marriage should be centered in love and obedience. A marriage is worthy of Jesus' presence.

The Bed (Is to be kept) Undefiled

Hebrew 13:4 states, "Marriage is honorable in all, and the bed (is to be kept) undefiled: but whoremongers and adulterers God will judge." This scripture begins by saying that every one of us need to respect and honor our marriage. The scripture states that the bed is to be kept undefiled. Let me give you three objects of defilement. (1) Conscience, (2) Fellowship, and (3) Flesh. What does it mean to be undefiled? I am glad you asked that question.

a) Undefiled means do not corrupt or ruin the conscience, fellowship or flesh.

b) It means do not damage somebody's reputation or good name with your conscience, fellowship or flesh.

c) It means do not make a holy, sacred thing or place no longer fit for ceremonial use due to your conscience, fellowship or flesh.

d) It means do not make something or somebody dirty or polluted due to your conscience, fellowship or flesh.

e) It means do not deprive a woman of her virginity if you are not married to her. Do not be the first to have sexual relations with a woman or a child usually outside of marriage, due to your conscience, fellowship or flesh.

> *I John 2: 16*
> *For all that is in the world, the lust*
> *of the flesh, and the lust of the eyes,*
> *and the pride of life, is not of the*
> *Father, but is of the world.*

Be careful. Do not let your earthly vision get in the way. Don't become so prideful and begin to lust with your eyes and flesh. This is not a God thing. This is a devil thing. Also be careful how you display your actions. People who are defiled are usually very narrow minded. When you marry, the bible states that you are to become one. You are a team now. Most narrow-minded people don't march with a team, but they march single because they are too narrow minded to march any other way. They choose to live a single life. They want to live a single life while yet married to you. I remember when my first husband use to play a particular record very loud quite a bit. I can still hear the melody and music. It would say, I'm living a single, single, single, life. He could have been trying to tell me something at that time but I just wasn't hearing it. If your husband chooses to live a single life while sleeping with you, then your bed becomes defiled. Your bed becomes tainted, which means your bed becomes polluted and contaminated. It means that your spouse is trying to corrupt you morally. It detracts from your reputation by associating yourself with something reprehensible. It gives you a foul scent. Tainted means to become spoil or become rotten and start stinking. Your bed will stink no matter how many times you change your sheets.

It is an imperfection that detracts from the quality of somebody or something. It is something that detracts from the purity or cleanliness of something. But God said the bed is to be kept undefiled. He also said to honor and respect your marriage. Some people don't have a clue about respect, not to mention respecting a marriage. I'd like to ask, "Who are you trying to impress when you defile the bed?" "Are you going to do it Gods way or the worlds' way?" If your bed is undefiled then your bed is not tainted. People who are undefiled are blessed. Undefiled is described in the act of marriage and should be taken very seriously. Your bed is to be kept undefiled. If you are going to do it God's way then keep your bed undefiled.

God Will Judge The Whoremongers

The scripture then adds that the whoremongers God will judge. Now if you call someone a whore then they will get offended right? It is an offensive word. The root word of whoremonger is whore. What is a whore? A whore is a promiscuous man or woman. The term whoremonger is used to refer to a sexually indiscriminate man or woman, especially one who frequents prostitutes. They are sexually indiscriminate! When you are indiscriminate then you are lacking judgement. You do not make careful choices. Prostitutes are not only walking the streets but there are some that go to church and look holy. Hello somebody! They also do things *hazardly random, haphazard*, or *confused*. That means that if you are a whoremonger then you are deficient or that there is a shortage in discernment or even good sense. You also lack the ability to form sound opinions and make sensible decisions. You are insufficient with a particular nutrient that is missing but needed for the body. A whoremonger is also someone who does not make careful choices. That means that they do not show caution and attention. They show no attention to accuracy and detail. Money or resources are spent or used wastefully and without thought. They are not watchful and protective about anything. They are full of anxious cares, meaning they are eager and wanting very much in a desperate or nervous way. When this happens then it produces anxiety. Anxiety produces feelings of fear, uncertainty, or nervousness.

A whoremonger is a man or a woman that is *hazardly random*. Hazard means that there is potential danger. If you are married to a whoremonger then be very careful and watch for signs. There could be a dangerous outcome and they could be taking risks to lose the marriage in order to gain something for themselves. Random means that they choose to do things that occur without a specific pattern, plan, or connection.

A whoremonger is also *haphazard*. What does that mean? It means that they do what they do in a way that has not been planned occasionally. The whoremonger is *confused*.

That means that they are unable to think intelligently. They sometimes want to be married to you and sometimes they don't. They are unable to think or reason clearly or to act sensibly. They are out of order. There is no logical or sensible order. On top of all that, these indiscriminate men and women frequent prostitutes or harlots on the streets and in the church. That means that they go after these types of men and women on a regular basis. It is habitual. They tend to go often to that place. We all know that when you engage in prostitution that sexual activity is involved for money, to get a bill paid, to get a happy meal or maybe just for company because you are so lonely. Don't sell yourself so cheap. You are worth more than that.

You need to know the characteristics of a harlot or prostitute. First of all they are shameless. They could care less what you or anybody else think about what they are doing. They could care less about breaking godly rules. They are untroubled or unaffected by shame, especially in situations when others will be shamed. Another characteristic is that they are enticing. They are very desirable and hard to resist. The harlot or the prostitute will roam the streets in the daytime or nighttime. Some of them are expensive and some of them are very cheap.

What are the evils of a harlot or prostitute?

First they profane God's name. God's holy name is dishonored. Why? The reason is no respect. Amos 2:7b states that fathers and sons sleep with the same women. That is no respect to God. This in itself dishonors Gods holy name. I remember when my spouse told me later in the marriage that he had slept with one of his sons' women. "Oh, player, player, is it like that?" I don't know how true it was but it frightened me that he would even speak such a thing. Some of us just allow anything to go on in our house. Wake up and stop sleeping so much. You can fool some people but you can't fool God. God knows and sees all. If this is you then you better get it together before it is too late. Sleeping from one bed to another with this person or that person dishonors God.

Secondly, the evils of a harlot or prostitute are connected with idolatry.

> *Exodus 34:15-16*
> *Lest thou make a covenant with the*
> *inhabitants of the land, and they go a*
> *whoring after their gods and do*
> *sacrifice unto their gods, and one call*
> *thee, and thou eat of his sacrifice.*
> *(verse 15)*
>
> *And thou take of their daughters unto thy*
> *sons, and their daughters go a whoring*
> *after their gods, and make thy sons go*
> *a whoring after their gods. (verse 16)*

These scriptures are saying that you agreed to fall away from the truth by your actions. You are committing adultery if you choose to chase whorish men and women. You have made a sacrifice to eat what the people of the world choose to eat. If you continue to eat what the world chooses to eat, then you will began to worship their gods. After you begin to worship their gods then you will marry their sons or daughters. After you marry their sons or daughters then the sons or daughters will begin to worship other gods. It will just be a continuous cycle. There will be a lot of evil influence. This causes you to forsake God. And because one chooses to worship other gods, then it causes a separation due to the falling away from the truth. This cycle will continue as long as you continue to worship other gods and fall away from the truth. You are falling away from the truth if you are sleeping around with this person and that person. Let me make it clear. You are to sleep only with your spouse. If he is NOT your spouse then you are NOT to sleep with him! If you continue to sleep around with this person or that person outside of your spouse then you are worshiping other gods. This is not acceptable to God. God said that there should not be any other gods before me. Falling away from the truth is also called apostasy. What causes apostasy? Satan, false teachers, perversion of scripture, persecution, unbelief, love of the world, hardened heart, and spiritual blindness cause apostasy.

Thirdly, the evils of the harlot or prostitute bring spiritual error.

> *Hosea 4:6-10*
> *My people are destroyed for the lack*
> *of knowledge because thou has rejected*
> *knowledge, I will also reject thee, that*
> *thou shalt be no priest to me: seeing*
> *thou hast forgotten the law of thy God,*
> *I will also forget thy children (verse 6)*
>
> *As they were increased, so they sinned*
> *against me: therefore will I change their*
> *glory into shame. (verse 7)*
>
> *They eat up the sin of my people, and they*
> *set their heart on their iniquity. (verse8)*
>
> *And there shall be, like people, like priest*
> *and I will punish them for their ways, and*
> *reward them their doings. (verse 9)*

For they shall eat, and not have enough:
they shall commit whoredom, and shall
not increase: because they have left off
to take heed to the Lord. (verse 10)

This passage of scriptures says plenty. It lets you know that sin is destructive. There is spiritual ignorance because you choose to reject it. People who are dominated by the spirit of error cannot see the error. Their mind is so clogged up with mess that they are convinced that they are right in what they are doing and everybody else is wrong. Some people simply despise instruction. Some really despise the word of God. And if one have actually heard the word of God, they act like they forgot what the word of God said. Some people actually glory in their wrong doings or wickedness. God said that He will change your glory into shame. God said that people actually set their hearts on doing evil. God said that He will punish you for your ways and you will be rewarded for the wrong you do. I don't know how nice the reward will be but you will find out if you continue in evil and wickedness. There are even those that teach the word of God and act like they forgot what the word of God said. God also said in the scripture, they shall eat and not have enough. They shall commit whoredom and shall not increase. Why? It is because you did not take heed to the Lord. It is because you did not take heed to the warning signs. It is because you are rebellious and stubborn and don't want to listen to the truth. You have fallen away from the truth.

We must pray that the Lord has greater influence on you than the enemy. Let's pray that your mind be renewed and that you study Gods word. Maybe then you will change and be committed to the life of Jesus Christ. As we are led by the

Holy Spirit we can help those who want to be helped and those who will listen so that they can come into the knowledge of the truth.

What causes spiritual error? Being Un-submissive, Un-teachable, defensive and argumentative are some of the reasons why there is spiritual error. Some people actually abuse their liberty, which causes them to become a servant of corruption and put them in bondage. Remember, these people cannot see the error because they think that what they are doing is natural or human and they ride on that.

I heard a co-worker say to a young lady that he didn't know any men that will not mess around or cheat on his wife. He was making a powerful statement that he believed that all men do it. I beg to differ. I told him that that was not true. He looked at me as if I was crazy. No, you are wrong and crazy if you think that every man or husband messes around or cheats with other woman while in a committed relationship. To prove his case, he used an example of a powerful Pastor with a very large congregation that did it. I told him, "Just because he did it does not make it right." I also said, "Just because he did it does not mean that everybody does it." He then asked me, "Why did he do it then?" I answered him by saying, "It was the spirit of error." He said, "What?" I said it again, "It was the spirit of error." That ended the whole conversation.

The Apostle Paul wrote, "But evil men and seducers shall wax worse and worse, deceiving, and being deceived" (2 Timothy 3:13). St Matthew wrote, "Jesus answered and said unto them, You do err, not knowing the scriptures, nor the power of God" (Matthew 22:29). Error produces misunderstanding. You can depart or fall away from the truth because of the ignorance of Gods word. There is spiritual blindness somewhere around you.

You can also fall away from dishonoring God because you don't know the power that God holds in his hands. If you stay in this state of mind then it will get worse and worse. You will begin to deteriorate. You will deceive others and they will deceive you. It will be a continuous cycle if you stay there. That's where the enemy wants you. He does not want you to be conscious of Gods word. So what the enemy does is work heavily on putting you to sleep. Have you ever noticed that every time you try to read the word of God that you fall asleep? I'll tell you what, it is not God putting you to sleep.

Getting back to what the co-worker said about the powerful Pastor, I don't know what caused this Pastor to get to this point. There could have been contention in the house. There could have been spiritual blindness. Some people even teach false doctrine and not sound doctrine only to stay in the spiritual error. Some people will find all kinds of ways to justify what they are doing to stay in the spiritual error. Some people will even use scriptures to justify what they are doing to stay in the spiritual error. Listen, Satan cannot help himself. He is so twisted that when the light of the word is shown on him, then he will always reveal himself for who and what he really is. Who and what is he? Satan is a thief. He is also a liar, a killer and a destroyer. The nature of the enemy is to destroy. The nature of God is to bring life. Ask God to forgive you for trusting in yourself and place your life completely in His hands. Promise God that you will live according to His word from this day forth. If you don't do it now then we know that you are glorying in what you are doing. It is still in you to do wrong. You need to change your stinking thinking. Repent now! Then turn from your wicked ways! Acknowledge God in all your ways and He will direct your path!

The scripture also stated that when you prosper or reach prosperity, you tend to change. Some people get a little funny when they get a little money. When God gives you the increase you look for man to give YOU the glory when they should be giving GOD the glory. This puts you in a dangerous state also. They eat up sin because they love sin and they have an evil heart. Sin is universal. That's why God said that He would punish the people for their deeds. It does not matter who you are. You can be the CEO of a major company, a popular Pastor of a large growing church, a Minister of a small storefront church, a bench member, a hard working man or woman or even the president. It does not matter who you are. And because you eat up sin, then there will always be disappointment because you will never be satisfied. You will never be satisfied! There shall not be increase if you choose not to take heed to the Lord and His rules or laws, which is the word of our Almighty God.

Finally, the evils of a harlot or prostitute will cause a divorce. If you continue to prostitute yourself and get out of the will of God, then this can cause a divorce. The prophet Jeremiah wrote, "And I saw, when for all the cases whereby backsliding Israel committed adultery I had put her away, and given her a bill of divorce, yet her treacherous sister Judah feared not, but went and played the harlot also" (Jeremiah 3:8). Some people don't fear at all being a harlot and they are very treacherous like Sister Judah! The kingdom of Israel was like an unfaithful wife (or husband) who became a prostitute. God knew that the kingdom of Israel had been unfaithful and committed many sins, yet He still hoped that she might come back to Him like many of us hope in a situation like this. Backsliding Israel didn't come back to Him, so He divorced her and sent them away.

Many times we know and see the signs of unfaithfulness but yet we wait and wait and hope and hope and it continues to get worse and worse. We then begin to deteriorate due to our spouse erring or falling away from the truth. Deteriorate means to make something worse in quality, value, or strength. We begin to lose our quality. We begin to lose our value. We begin to get weak. Finally, we divorce them and put them away like God did the Israelites. Now if you are in a situation like this, then don't you start to prostitute yourself because your spouse is doing it. I've seen that happen a lot. "Well since he's doing it, I am going to do it to." "Two can play that game!" NOT! Don't do it. Depart if you must but don't play the same game.

God Will Judge The Adulterers

The bible states that God will judge adulterers. What is adultery? It is voluntary sexual intercourse with someone other than one's husband or wife. God commands that no one is to commit adultery. If you do it anyway, then you are breaking Gods laws. God commands that you do not commit adultery. There is a penalty for committing adultery. It is punishable by death.

> *Leviticus 20: 10-12*
> *And the man that committeth adultery with another man's wife, even he that committeth adultery with his neighbors wife, the adulterer and the adulteress shall surely be put to death. (verse 10)*

And the man that lieth with his father's wife hath uncovered his father's nakedness: both of them shall surely be put to death; their blood shall be upon them. (verse 11)

And if a man that lie with his daughter in law, both of them shall surely be put to death: they have wrought confusion, their blood shall be upon them. (verse 12)

The fact that God commanded us not to commit adultery is very serious even though people take it so lightly. If any man have sex with another man's wife, both you and the woman will be put to death with your spiritual self. The enemy has now put you in sleep mode even though you didn't realize it. Having sex with your father's wife disgraces God. Listen, it isn't natural for you to have sex with your daughter in law. The bible states that both of you will be put to death. Now we know for sure it will be a spiritual death, but at the same time it can cause a physical death. So be ever so careful and don't take it so lightly. You may think you are getting away with the wrong you are doing but God sees and knows all. God is omniscient, meaning He has infinite knowledge. God is omnipotent meaning He has infinite power. He is the Almighty God that is in control of nature, nations and all things. God is omnipresent meaning His presence is universal. He is all knowing and all-powerful and He is everywhere at the same time. So what's done in the dark will come to the light because you will be judged.

Philippians 2: 10-11
That at the name of Jesus every knee
should bow, of things in heaven, and
things in earth, and things under the
earth; (verse 10)

And that every tongue should confess
that Jesus Christ is Lord, to the glory
of God the Father. (verse 11)

God will judge you and you need to know that whether you get it together or not. If you are not bowing down right now to God you will one day. Why do you say that? I say that because every knee shall bow and every tongue shall confess that Jesus is Lord. God will look at your life's journey and judge you accordingly. So get it together. Why not confess that Jesus is Lord right now and choose the life that God has planned for you. All of you that are committing adultery today have been put to sleep by the enemy and you need to wake up! The enemy loves to keep you in sleep mode but there is a way out if you choose to get out of this type of situation. Some of you act like you forgot that you even made a covenant with your spouse. So now you are considered to be a covenant breaker because you have gotten on the wrong path. You took a wrong turn somewhere because you fell asleep. Do me a favor, WAKE UP! The reason I say that is because you are dead asleep right now! If you decide to keep sleeping with the enemy by committing adultery then it will make you poor. I'm speaking of poor in spirit, poor in wisdom, and poor in peace and joy. It will break you. Oh yes, you will be broken. As long as you continue to keep company with harlots and prostitutes you will lose substance. You don't have to be walking the streets to be characterized as a prostitute. You don't have to be in a strip club either to be characterized as a prostitute. You can read your bible on a regular basis and go to church every Sunday and still be considered to be a prostitute or harlot. The so-called Christians that go to church every Sunday can be just as treacherous as anybody else that is of the world.

The book of Proverbs reads, "Such is the way of an adulteress woman, she eateth, and wipeth her mouth, and saith, I have done no wickedness" (Proverbs 30:20). Why do she say that? I'll tell you why, because of her self-righteousness and self-deception. You are deceiving yourself if you think that there is nothing wrong with you sleeping around so freely, whether married or not. Stop eating all that junk food while wiping your mouth and saying, "I didn't do anything wrong." Oh yes you did, so stop deceiving yourself and wake up! If you continue to do it anyway, then you are considered to be a harlot and an evil person. Let's just keep it real. Can we talk? Repent now and change from your wicked ways! If not then trust me, God will humble you.

I have a question. Where is your heart? Do you even know? You need to search and find it. Has it been taken away from you? Hosea wrote, "Whoredom and wine and new wine take away the heart" (Hosea 4:11). Back in the day when I used to drink and sleep around, I could care less that I hurt people in the process because it was all about me. All I wanted was my drink and a man to keep me company. The scripture says that whoring around takes away the heart. If this is you then you will at times say anything or do anything that can wound other people. You have no heart so that doesn't bother you. I didn't realize at the time that I was considered to be a harlot or prostitute due to my actions. My heart was a heart of stone. I became so heartless. I didn't see anything wrong with what I was doing because I was living in deception. And if anybody stepped to me talking crazy, I would get him or her told or even cuss them out. I must say though, I was truly penalized for my own actions. That's why when people look at me on my job or any other place like I am crazy because I don't have a man right now. Guess what? I could care less what they think about me because I choose to wait on God this time. It is not that I don't want a man in my life and its not that I can't get a man. Its just that after all I have been through, I decided that I will not rush into another relationship knowing that I am not ready and he is not ready either. I don't just want any man so God had to give me a new heart. Instead of a heart of stone, I needed a heart of flesh. Even though I was alright with it in the past, it now irritates my spirit to hear people brag on being in a relationship with Tom, Dick and Harry or Sally, Sue and Captain Silly. Why? It is because God gave me a new heart. It is because I don't want anyone to go through what I've been through. It was very damaging and painful. There is nothing cute about it. It corrupts your land. It corrupts your mind. It corrupts your environment. It also justifies divorce if you are married.

> *St. Matthew 19:7-8*
> *They say unto him, Why did Moses then*
> *command to give a writing of divorcement,*
> *and to put her away. (verse 7)*
>
> *He saith unto them, Moses because of the*
> *hardness of your hearts suffered you to put*
> *away your wives: but from the beginning*
> *it was not so. (verse 8)*

Listen, the Pharisees asked Jesus, "Why did Moses say that a man could write out divorce papers and send his wife away?" Jesus replied, "Because you are so heartless! That's why Moses allowed you to divorce your wife. But from the beginning God did not intend for it to be that way. Jesus said that if your wife has not committed some terrible sexual sin, you must not divorce her to marry someone else. If you do then you are considered to be unfaithful." If you commit adultery then it could end in hell.

> *Proverbs 7:24-27*
> *Hearken (listen) unto me now therefore,*
> *O you children, and attend to the words of*
> *my mouth. (verse 24)*
>
> *Let not thine heart decline to her ways, go*
> *not astray in her paths. (Do not start*
> *wandering and be misled by this type of*
> *woman. The enemy is setting a trap for*
> *you so be very careful) (verse 25)*
>
> *For she hath cast down many wounded: yea,*
> *many strong men have been slain by her.*
> *(verse 26)*
>
> *Her house is the way to hell, going down to*
> *the chambers of death. (verse 27)*

Most people make a conscious choice to commit an evil act. Some people are masters of justification. Some people want success so bad that they are blind to the wrong that they are doing. Some people lust after money so much that they don't realize the evil acts that they are doing in order to get it. Some women think it is normal to get money from someone else's husband in exchange for what they call good sex. These women use sex as a weapon. Come on, wake up!

225

I can see some of you walking around smiling and saying, "He wants me." "Look at him, he's hot!" No, he just wants your body! Not only is he disrespecting you but you are also disrespecting yourself. Many times it is for the love of money. Money is not evil but the LOVE of money is the root of all evil. That means that you must have right relationship with money. Some people want out of their marriage so badly that they are willing to kill their families with all the evil acts that they are committing. It is all over the news. They may not say it but their actions show it. This can kill your family. Some want out so badly that they are willing to steal someone else's identity. That is crazy!

Do you even know who you are? Are you a man or woman of God? I hope that you are not a con man or woman. If you are then the enemy, who put you to sleep, is influencing you. If you must con someone to marry you then the enemy who has put you to sleep is influencing you. Maybe you just like a lot of attention. Maybe you are getting a little lonely. Trust me if you don't watch it, wanting so much attention and feeling so lonely can get you in a lot of trouble. The flesh is calling for attention. It is saying, "Attention, I need some assistance right now!" A con man or woman always wants to be the center of attention. They always want to be on stage. They could probably get an award for acting. It is not about you. You are not the star. Jesus Christ is our superstar! If this is you, then please wake up because a big Mack Truck is headed your way. If this is you then you are headed for destruction. Satan loose him and let him go! Satan Loose her and let her go! Right now in the name of Jesus! Father I thank you that someone will receive this word and decide to wake up out of sleep. I pray that they will stop sleeping with the enemy. I pray that after gaining knowledge that you will finally take off the grave clothes. If you do not wake up and come out of the grave clothes then you will die.

Put Away

St. Matthew 19:8 states, "because of the hardness of your hearts suffered (allowed) you to put away your wives." What causes the heart to harden? What causes someone that once loved you to harden his or her heart? What causes them to be so hard on you? It is as if they are addictive in inflicting pain. This is hard to bear and hard to endure. When they have hardened their hearts they show little or no sympathy, compassion, or gentleness. They are insensitive. It is as if they are bitter and they resent you. I remember feeling like my spouse hated me. Even though he said with his lips that he loved me, his actions didn't show it. This becomes hard to understand. In some cases when they are hard on you then it makes them feel mighty and in control. In some cases they may use a lot of force or violence. This is real and true. It is the cold hard facts. When they are hard on you, then they will also become visually harsh. If this happens, then this is usually a sign that they are wandering while you are wondering what happened. The enemy wants you to wander to put you in sleep mode. It will make you wonder if in fact they ever really cared. You may even think to yourself that they never really loved me or cared for me. You may say, "If they really loved me and cared for me, then why did they wander in the first place?"

What causes a person to wander? A person will wander from place to place because they are without purpose or without a known destiny. They are without vision. They are lost. They begin to daydream so they lost the ability to concentrate on or listen to a particular voice. The bible states,

"My sheep know my voice and a stranger they will not follow." So since you are daydreaming, you lost the ability to think, speak, or write in an organized and coherent way. When the enemy puts you to sleep then you don't know what to think. You don't know what to say. You can barely even write a note without being confused. You will be unorganized. If this is you then you have become incoherent. You are sleeping with the enemy and that is where he wants you. You need to stop sleeping with the enemy! Wake up! Deliver us oh God!

Put away means to confine somebody. It means to put somebody in prison or a psychiatric state of mind. If your heart is hardened and you put your wife or husband away by committing adultery and abusing him or her, then this can cause someone to die. I don't know about you but I don't want to die. I want to live. I'm sure that Cain's brother Abel didn't want to die either. Cain was sleeping with the enemy when he killed his own brother Abel. God said in his word, "Thou shall not kill." There is a penalty you have to pay for sin. Sin separates. Genesis 4:16 reads, "And Cain went out from the presence of the Lord." After the sin was committed, he began to wander. After he killed his loved one then he began to wander. He wandered from the presence of God. This is a dangerous state to be in. If you are not careful, this can cause you to lose your mind or focus due to wandering and daydreaming. Talking about, "How did this happen?" "How did I get here?"

When you are put away then you become the opponent because of opposition. Maybe you are living in opposition to the word of God because your loved one put you away. You need to know that put away also means to beat an opponent decisively like in a sporting event. You can be beaten with words or beaten physically. Neither one is appropriate.

Whether you are beaten physically or mentally with words or actions they both hurt just as bad. There should never be any violence in your relationship. No one should ever deal with you treacherously. In order to have a successful marriage you must communicate properly. You must remember the laws of sowing and reaping. Your words are seeds. They will either bring a good crop or a bad crop. So if you or your spouse keeps threatening infidelity or divorce then you must remember that there is power in spoken words. The power of life and death is in the tongue.

When you are put away then this creates a distance of time or space between the two of you. When you are firm in putting him or her away, then there is a realization that it didn't just happen. It requires great energy, effort and often-physical exertion. It takes all that to achieve an evil act such as committing adultery or sleeping with the enemy by killing someone. Yes words can destroy you and hurt you. The enemy wants you to keep sleeping with him and die. Listen, I realize that it really doesn't matter what they say or do to me. It does matter what I say or do to myself. You will never die by what they say to you. The fact of the matter is do you believe what they say about you when they put you down or say all manner of evil against you? You do not have to receive that. The enemy wants to bring a curse on the house. His mission is to divide and conquer. Mark 3:25 reads, "And if a house be divided against itself, that house cannot stand." When there is division in the house, it weakens the relationship. Don't give into the enemy devices. Don't become arrogant or disobedient because of how you are being treated but keep your humble attitude if you can. You need to know that God will fight your battle. Make sure you hear from God on what you should do and don't take matters into your own hands.

Chapter 19
BROKEN AGREEMENT

Malachi 2:14-17
Yet you say wherefore? Because the Lord
hath been witness between thee and the wife
of thy youth, against whom thou hast dealt
treacherously: yet is she thy companion, and
the wife of thy covenant. (verse 14)

Some unfaithful men want to know why is God not pleased with them. They say, "What did I do?" "What did I say?" It is because God knows and have witnessed all the unfaithful men that's been unfaithful to the wives that they have married and made a covenant with. He has witnessed you dealing treacherously with your wife. You became a traitor. You betrayed her trust, confidence and faith. Why did you do that? That means that you were unfaithful. You became perilous by involving hidden dangers or hazards. There was just a lot of deceitfulness going on.

You promised to love and cherish her. Now it is not like you go looking for reasons to get a divorce but lets keep it real. If you make a covenant or agreement with a monster then you are bound to break the agreement. You promised to be my covering. I realized that if you marry a man that has no relationship with God then you will not be covered properly. You promised to accompany me and spend time with me and you even are supposed to be my friend. The problem is now you have broken your promises. You broke the agreement. So you are working seven days a week now. Hey hey you're the man now, huh? You don't have time for your wife and children anymore. I literally experienced my husband working overtime all the time. Never having time for God, church, wife or children. Honey, you can't work all the time. You need some balance. You need to get some manna from heaven. So God will humble you and cause you to hunger. He will make you know that it is not always about the bread (money) you make. It is not always about the bread you eat naturally. Luke 4:4 reads, "And Jesus answered him, saying, It is written, that man shall not live by bread alone, but by every word of God." You must have a spiritual life and the word of God should be your food also. Go ahead and make all the bread you want but you can't leave God out. Do not fall for Satan's temptation. God is the reason that you even have a job in the first place. Now you want to leave God out? If this is you that is working all the time, and there is nothing wrong with working, but you are living an unbalanced life. The only time that the wife and children get to see you is when you are asleep or when you come home for sex. You better wake up and smell the coffee. It takes two to work a marriage. No not one!

The enemy will offer you earthly honor by taking you up into a high mountain. The enemy will give you earthly vision by giving you satanic power. The devil wants you to fall down and worship him as he offered Jesus the same thing. You must resist the devil. Luke 4:8 reads, "And Jesus answered and said unto him, Get thee behind me Satan: for it is written, Thou shall worship the Lord thy God, and him only shall thou serve." Use the word of God as a weapon against Satan. Worship and serve God.

And did not he make one? Yet had he the
residue of the spirit. And wherefore one?
that he might seek a godly seed. Therefore
take heed to your spirit and let none deal
treacherously against the wife of his youth.
Malachi 2:15

Didn't God create you to become as one with your wife? Oneness equal unity. Unity is the state of being one. It is the combining or joining of separate things or entities to form one. It is combining your thoughts together. It is combining your ways together. It is the harmony of opinion, interest, or feeling. You should compliment each other. You should respect one another. You should build one another up. When this happens this will cause you both to become whole and complete. For instance, an action of a play should be limited to one plot. This is the unity of action. You both have important roles to play as a wife and a husband. It should be limited to one plot or plan. That plan should be to build and not tear down.

There should be an architectural plan of building. You must come up with a plan to build on the relationship. You cannot build with a liar and a cheat. So you can't build with an animal, monster or beast. Be very careful whom you choose. Hopefully as a believer you are going to seek and choose a godly seed. God should be the head of this plan. Why do you say that? The reason is because God is into building. Oh yes, God is the Master Builder! He is the Supreme Architect!

Unit is the root word of unity. A unit is a single person that is whole. Make sure that you are whole before you unite with anybody. Make sure you are complete. There should be nothing missing and nothing broken. As a believer, before you decide to make a covenant or agreement, make sure you seek and choose a godly seed. Therefore watch your spirit and consider your ways so that neither one of you can be dealt with treacherously. Honey, don't you ever marry just for money because it won't work.

> *For the Lord, the God of Israel, said that he*
> *hateth putting away: for one covereth*
> *violence with his garment, said the Lord*
> *of hosts: therefore take heed to your spirit,*
> *that you deal not treacherously. (verse 16)*

> *You have wearied the Lord with your words,*
> *Yet you say, Wherein have we wearied him?*
> *when you say, Every one that do evil is good*
> *in the sight of the Lord, and he delighteth in*
> *them; or, Where is the God of judgement?*
> *(verse 17)*

God hates divorce or putting away. The Lord also knows when you try to cover up violence. That's why God said, you need to take heed to your spirit. Take heed to your spirit so that you don't deal violently or treacherously with anyone. Why do you violate someone who wants to be married and wants to live a godly life? Why do you string them along when you know you are violent or treacherous. Why do you get in relationship with people to purposely destroy them? God is watching you! Your violent or treacherous words are making God tired. Then the people begin to scoff or mock the Lord by saying, "How did we make the Lord tired?" Then they say, "Everybody that do evil is good in the sight of the Lord." Then they say, "God gets great pleasure in them, He likes it, if not then where is the God of judgement?" Judgement will come if you don't watch your spirit and consider your ways.

BROKEN AGREEMENT

Haggai 1:5-8
Now therefore thus saith, the LORD of hosts;
Consider your ways. (verse 5)

You have sown much, and bring in little; you
eat, but you have not enough; you drink, but
you are not filled with drink; you clothe you,
but there is none warm; And he that earneth
wages to put it into a bag with holes (verse 6)

Thus saith the LORD of hosts, Consider your
ways. (verse 7)

Go up to the mountain, and bring wood, and
build the house; and I will take pleasure in it
and I will be glorified, said the LORD.
(verse 8)

These passages of scriptures are saying, give careful thought to your ways. If you mess up and ruin the house then you will have to rebuild. It is not an easy thing to do unless you include God. Don't ruin the house by lying and cheating. Don't ruin the house by committing adultery. Don't ruin the house by belittling anyone. Don't ruin the house by being so monstrous. It will not be easy to rebuild a relationship when a lot of heartache and pain is involved. The bible says that you plant much but you harvest little. You wonder why there is a struggle? It is because your house, which is supposed to be the temple of God, has not been rebuilt yet. It is because you may have planted bad seeds. It is because that you hurry off to build your own monster looking houses, while the temple of God is still in ruins. It is because you are too busy doing your own thing. You have gotten caught up with the cares of this world. It is because the enemy has tricked you. That's why your harvest fails. It is like all your hard work will be for nothing. It is because you lack respect for the Lords temple, which showed that you lack respect for the Lord himself. If this happens then God can refuse to bless you.

God used Haggai the prophet, to get the message to the people. Has God ever used anybody in your life to get a message to you? If so, then I hope you obeyed God. You must give careful thought to your ways. Work on the temple, then the Lord will bless you and make you prosperous. Let God fill your house with His Glory. You must work hard in order to build the house. You must work hard to build the temple of God. You must pray and seek Gods face. Go to the mountains. Look to the hills from which comes your help. Your help comes from the Lord. If you are the type of person that thinks that you don't need any help, then it just won't work. Help us Lord, Jesus. We need your help oh God!

If you choose to unite, then a common interest or concern should unify you. Look to see if they have the same values that you have. Remember you will be combining each of your qualities. Think about it. What qualities does he or she have? What qualities do you have? I have noticed that two dominant people normally clash. They may bump heads a lot. That's why it is so important to choose wisely. You should be united in harmony and agreement. A union is a result of bringing people together that are whole to form a whole.

If you have a family reunion then you don't just tell the family we are going to have a family reunion so let's get together. You have to come up with a plan. You have to set a date. You have to set a place. You have to set the time. That means that you are going to have to labor. Why do you say that? The reason is because there is a lot of work involved in bringing the family together. A marriage is work. Now things may or may not work out the way that you planned it but keep trying. A marriage is not for wimps. A marriage is not for lazy people either. If you are a lazy person and don't want to work, then don't get married. If you see the residue of this spirit on the person that you have decided to marry then please slow down and don't get married just yet. You must be creative and productive when God gives you the godly seed you have been waiting for. You must be willing to sow into the relationship. Before you enter into the marriage do you even see the fruit of the spirit? What are the fruit of the spirit? It is love, joy, peace, longsuffering (patience), gentleness, goodness, faith, meekness and temperance (self-control). Are you bearing good fruit or not? Are they bearing good fruit or not?

God gives seed to the sower. Once God gives you the seed then you must not stop there. You should be fruitful or productive and multiply it. You got to do some planting. Plant love, kindness, gentleness, etc. You need to know that whatever you plant that a crop will come. Depending on what you plant determines the kind of crop you get. Hopefully it is good crop and not a bad crop. You got to do some cultivating in order for the relationship to grow. That means that you have to do some nurturing in order to improve or develop the growth. This may come by way of more education or training from our Almighty God. God can even teach you how to communicate with one another. Communication is very important in a successful marriage. This may come by way of learning to operate in the fruit you were once weak in. You also need to do some watering to keep the plant alive. You must be creative and work it. Work it, work it, work it!

Why not set dates on occasions with your spouse and do something special. You should set a special place to live that you both agree on. You should set time for the family from your busy schedules sometimes. You might as well join the labor union. What is a labor union? A labor union is an organization of wage earners that is set up to serve and advance its members interests in terms of wages, benefits, and working hours and conditions. You must work your marriage. You will earn wages when you take time out for one another and build one another up. You will get benefits when you serve one another. You should all ready be set up to serve. If you do this then the marriage can advance with interest. Learn to keep your marriage interesting. There is a couple that I admire that has been married for a long time. The husband said that he lets nothing get in the way of taking his wife out to dinner every Friday. Now this may not work with your schedule but they came up with this plan and it worked for them.

Chapter 20
GOD IS FAITHFUL

Have you ever trusted in someone that let you down? Maybe you trusted in your parents and they let you down. Maybe you trusted in your children and they let you down. Maybe you trusted in your Pastor and he or she let you down. Why? The reason is because they are human with imperfections. But with these imperfections are they striving to do better? Are they allowing the enemy to constantly influence them or are they walking in the spirit and seeking God for guidance? So you thought you found the love of your life, huh? Some people believe in happily ever after endings. Some people even believe that some hearts are destined to be together. In some cases this may be true while in other cases some relationships could become blessing blockers.

I had my own hang up with destiny. My husband and I immersed in conflict and misunderstanding. This kept us from working together on the marriage. This kept us from working things out. We didn't realize that we could have resolved our misunderstandings and conflict by committing and serving one another while serving God. Our flesh was controlling us in many ways. There were some cases when we left God out and walked totally in the flesh. There were times that we trusted our own self rather than God. I have learned that there will not be a successful marriage without the main ingredient, Jesus. I have learned that God should be the focus of my life and my spouse's life in order to have a successful marriage. I have learned that communication is vital. We must learn how to speak properly to one another. A marriage is wedlock. When you wed, a woman wants to feel a sense of security and safety. She wants to know what kind of relationship is she going to be locked into. Is it safe and secure? How can a woman feel safe if she is being put down a lot? How can a woman feel safe when she is being abused physically and mentally? How can a woman feel safe if a man strings her along and treat her treacherously and with violence? How can a woman feel safe if she is married to an adulterer? How can a woman feel safe if he is never home and never spend any time with you or the children? How can a woman feel safe when he is dealing drugs and doing drugs? How can a woman feel safe when she is abandoned? How can a woman feel safe when she is constantly being disrespected? How can a woman feel safe when she is seeking the kingdom of God and he is NOT? How can a woman feel safe when he is constantly lying and cheating? How can a woman feel safe when he is constantly showing hatred towards her? When you decide to marry, God should be the center of your relationship. If not, then your marriage will not be successful.

Listen, my sisters, your marriage will not be successful if you trust in your own strength to make the marriage work. If you make flesh your arm then it will not be successful. If a man's heart is turned away from God while you are serving God, then the marriage will not be successful. Be careful not to bring a curse on the house or yourself. Trust is not to be placed in man or you.

> *Jeremiah 17:5-6*
> *Thus said the Lord: Cursed be the man that*
> *trusteth in man, (or yourself) and maketh*
> *flesh his arm, and whose heart departeth*
> *from the Lord. (verse 5)*

For he shall be like the heath in the desert,
and shall not see when good cometh; but
shall inhabit the parched places in the
wilderness, in a salt land and not inhabited.
(verse 6)

Some people trust in their own human strength. This is considered to be a false trust because you are forsaking God. God said that He will put a curse on those who turn from Him and trust in their own human strength. Also to those whose heart has gone away from God. There will be a spiritual drought. There will be spiritual loss. There will be dry places. If you place your trust in human strength, then you will dry up like a bush in a salty desert soil, where nothing can grow. Now that should make you feel a little salty or bothered. Trust in God because He is faithful.

Jeremiah 17:7-8
Blessed is the man that trusted in the Lord,
and whose hope the Lord is. (verse 7)

For he shall be as a tree planted by the waters,
and that spreadeth out her roots by the river,
and shall not see when heat cometh, but her
leaf shall be green; and shall not be careful
in the year of drought, neither shall cease
from yielding fruit. (verse 8)

If you put your trust in God, then you will be blessed. There is hope in God but you must put your trust in Him because He is faithful. You will be like a tree planted because you are rooted and grounded in God. If you put your trust in God then when drought comes you will still yield fruit. You shall not stop yielding fruit in the year of drought. In other words, love, kindness, gentleness, self-control, etc. should still be there. Why? It is because you are yielding spiritual fruit. And as long as you continue to trust God, you will have an unfading life.

Trust means to put one's confidence in. Trust is not to be placed in man's strength or your strength. Let me give you some examples of how and what we may put our trust in. Some people trust weapons such as guns. Some people actually put their trust in their gun to save them or to get what they want. They also think that it ends there. You should not trust in a gun and neither will it save you. At one time in my life I thought a gun was going to save me from my husband. If you are dealing with a demonic force or spirit then there is plenty where that came from. The demonic forces and demonic spirits will not stop there. Shooting someone will not solve the problem. Honey you will be shooting for days if that's the case. I thought that if I killed my husband then all of my troubles would be over. I thought that I would stop him from hurting anybody else. God had to wake me up out of that terrible nightmare. The enemy really had me in sleep mode. The Lord himself had to wake me up out of sleep!

Some people put their trust in their wealth. You are not to put your trust in your wealth and riches. Don't boast about it either. Your wealth and riches cannot redeem you or your brother. Wealth and riches cannot save your marriage even though it seems to soothe some of your pain. So you thought that your power and wealth could save you huh? I don't think so! If you think that then you will be captured and wiped out by the enemy. In this case you will not escape destruction. Remember that after you get finished spending all that money, you will still have to face reality. On the other hand, lets not put people down because they have money either. A lot of them labored and gave a lot of time to get where they are today. What do you spend your time doing?

You should not put all your confidence in every leader because they cannot always help you. Your help comes from the Lord. Leaders can and will make mistakes but that doesn't mean that you have to be so hard on them either. Let's pray for our leaders. Pray that they acknowledge God in all their ways so that God can direct their path. Pray that they have some sense of direction by following God. You should not place your trust or confidence in your own works. Why do I say that? I say that because without God we are nothing. Finally I'd like to add that you should not put your confidence in ones own righteousness. This could get you in trouble by trying to have it your own way and not Gods way. There are so many people that prefer to do it their own way rather than Gods way. Many times it is because of the way that they were raised and they choose not to change.

Now there is someone that you should place your trust in. He is someone who is always faithful and just. Who is that? It is God that is always faithful and just. First and foremost you should trust in the name of God. God is our help and our shield. Psalm 33:21 reads, "For our heart shall rejoice in him, because we have trusted in his holy name." Call on Him! When you are dealing with the issues of life and it began to weigh you down, why not call on the name of the Lord. If you need a healing, call on Him! If you need your heart fixed, call on Him! If you need deliverance, your mind regulated, comforting, a job, etc., all you have to do is call on Him! I guarantee you that God will see you through. The believer should always trust in God and His word. Did you know that the word of God is God?

St. John 1:1-5
In the beginning was the Word, and the Word
was with God, and the Word was God.
(verse 1)

The same was in the beginning with God.
(verse 2)

All things were made by him, and without
him was not anything made that was made.
(verse 3)

In him was life, and the life was the light of
men. (verse4)

And the light shineth in darkness; and the
darkness comprehended it not. (verse5)

From the beginning was the one who is called the Word. The Word was with God from the beginning. Christ is the Word. Christ is eternal. Christ is divine. Christ is the life. Christ is the light. Christ is the creator. With Christ you will be enlightened. With this Word God created all things. Nothing was made without the Word. So the Word must make you because without the Word you will not be made. You can try to make yourself but you will not be made the right way until the Word of God makes you. Everything that was created received its life from God. Light can put the darkness out but the darkness cannot put the light out. The light will always outshine the darkness. If you read Gods Word then He will talk to you. And God said, "Let there be light" and there was light. There is power in spoken words. There is power in Gods Word.

The Word is spiritual food for the believer. It gives you a standard of conduct because we don't always know how to act when we are hit with heartache and pain. It is a source of new life. The more you read Gods Word, you will learn that you haven't really been living like you could and should. The Word gives you a source of joy. It will guide you. It will cause you to have restraints so that you can control yourself. Some people cannot control what they are doing because they have no power and no Word. They don't have any word to stand on because they are empty. The Word purifies. It also causes a spiritual cleansing. Listen, we all need to be cleansed on a daily basis. We must bathe our bodies daily. Likewise we must bathe in the Word daily to cleanse the body. I guarantee you that you will begin to have such a good smelling fragrance to the body of Christ. It will cause you not to wander from His commandments. Gods Word is very important. You must place your trust in His Word and His Holy Name. Our Lord and Savior Jesus Christ is all powerful so He can fix any situation. He is all knowing so He sees everything that you are facing or going through and is concerned about you. He is also ever present and eternal. As long as you place your trust in the faithful one, God, and stand on His promises, then when the enemy comes up against you, all you have to say is, "IT IS WRITTEN!" You must believe that God can bring you out or deliver you from terrible situations. Do not try to force Gods hand. God will do it in His timing and NOT yours. He is an on time God anyway. Oh yes He is!

ARE YOU SLEEPING WITH THE ENEMY? IF SO, THEN WAKE UP AND STOP SLEEPING WITH THE ENEMY!

CONCLUSION

Philippians 3:13-14
Brethren, I count not myself to have
apprehended: but this one thing I do,
forgetting those things which are behind,
and reaching forth unto those things
which are before, (verse 13)

I press toward the mark for the prize of
the high calling of God in Christ Jesus.
(verse 14)

My friends, I do not feel that I have already arrived. This one thing I do know. I am forgetting those things that are behind me. There is spiritual progress and I have a Holy Ambition to achieve. I am spiritually striving to reach for those things that are before me. I encourage you to do the same thing. No you have not arrived. Forget about those things that are behind you and strive to reach those things that are before you spiritually. You should have a Holy Ambition to achieve also. So press. I press toward the mark of the high calling of God in Christ Jesus. There is a high calling of God on your life. There is a high calling of God on my life. I'm speaking of the Christian calling. I'm speaking of the Christian race. It is time for us to grow up to reach spiritual maturity. We have a goal to reach so that we could win the prize of being called into the heavenlies. It may be a struggle sometimes but we must press anyhow. God Bless You.

This message is not to condemn anyone but this message is to give understanding of life's struggles if you choose wrongly. Now God I repent and pray that you continue to touch me as you did with the woman with the issue of blood. Continue to use me Lord in a mighty way. Thank you God for all that you've done and all that you're going to do in my life. Continue to build me up into the woman of God that you would have me to be. These things I ask in Jesus name, Amen.

Author Contact

Sheri D. Smith
P. O. Box 4104
Fairview Heights, Illinois 62208

Email Address:
sheridsmith@hotmail.com

You're welcome to send your prayer requests. Please include your testimony and indicate how this book has blessed you when you write.